That Patchwork Place®

Quilting Up a Storm

*New Ways to Interpret a
Classic Block Design*

Lydia Quigley

Credits

Editorial Director **Kerry I. Hoffman**
Technical Editor **Sharon Rose**
Managing Editor **Greg Sharp**
Copy Editor **Tina Cook**
Proofreader **Melissa Riesland**
Design Director **Judy Petry**
Text and Cover Designer **Amy Shayne**
Production Assistants **Shean Bemis**
Dani Ritchardson
Illustrator **Laurel Strand**
Illustration Assistant **Lisa McKenney**
Photographer **Brent Kane**
Photography Assistant **Richard Lipshay**

Quilting Up a Storm:
New Ways to Interpret a Classic Block Design
© 1996 by Lydia Quigley
That Patchwork Place, Inc., PO Box 118
Bothell, WA 98041-0118 USA

Library of Congress Cataloging-in-Publication Data

Quigley, Lydia.
Quilting up a storm : new ways to interpret a classic block
design / Lydia Quigley.
p. cm.
ISBN 1-56477-138-5
1. Patchwork—Patterns. 2. Quilting—Patterns.
3. Storms in art. I. Title.
TT835.Q49 1196
746.46—dc20
95-49045
CIP

Acknowledgments

No book gets written without help
from special people. Thanks to:

All my friends who supported and
encouraged me along the way.

Elizabeth Lake, for encouraging me
to write this book and for her support throughout.

Pam MacGregor, for her help in
quilting "Floral Fanta-Sea."

My kindest critics, sons Brandon and Evan Quigley,
who always tell me my quilts are great.

Printed in the United States of America
01 00 99 98   6 5 4

MISSION STATEMENT

WE ARE DEDICATED TO PROVIDING QUALITY
PRODUCTS AND SERVICES THAT INSPIRE CREATIVITY.

WE WORK TOGETHER TO
ENRICH THE LIVES WE TOUCH.

That Patchwork Place is a financially responsible ESOP company.

Contents

Preface

When I made my first Storm at Sea quilt, I dutifully used templates and marked and cut out all the required pieces. As I admired my finished quilt, I realized the exciting potential of the Storm at Sea pattern. I was eager to work further with the design, but I was not so eager to mark and cut individual template pieces. I decided there had to be a way to piece the design without them.

I have been quilting and teaching for a number of years, and my focus is on trying new techniques that make the quiltmaking process fast, fun, and above all, accurate. I avoid marking and cutting out templates whenever possible, since rotary-cutting techniques provide quicker and easier options. For Storm at Sea, I knew that parts of the design, like the square with four right-angle corners, were easy to make without templates—but how was I to get those sharp points without them? Rotary-cut squares and rectangles, along with an accurately marked sewing line, solved that problem. And so the idea was born.

Introduction

The most interesting aspect of the Storm at Sea design is the illusion of movement it creates. Depending upon your use of color and value, waves may ripple or stars may twinkle across the surface of your quilt.

The variety of designs in this book illustrate Storm at Sea's endless possibilities. The patterns range from traditional Storm at Sea designs to unique variations that share basic construction techniques but have little else in common with Storm at Sea.

The quilts in this book are made with what are generally referred to as "quick" cutting and piecing techniques, many of which are now commonplace in the quilting world. I find these techniques to be far more accurate than templates and easier to use. All you need is a sewing machine, a rotary cutter and mat, a ruler with ⅛" markings, and a sharp pencil or two.

Fabrics

Choose only good quality, 100% cotton fabrics. They are the easiest to work with and give the best results. Why complicate your life?

You can make Storm at Sea from as few as three fabrics or from as many as you find in your scrap bag. I like to use a wide variety of fabrics in my quilts. I think it makes them interesting, and it's more fun to choose ten different reds than just one. I usually buy no more than a half-yard of any particular fabric unless I want to use it for background or borders.

I choose the color schemes for my quilts in different ways. Sometimes the design indicates a color scheme, such as the brightly colored tropical fish and blue background in "School of Fish" on page 26. At other times, I choose a multicolored print and add appropriate coordinating colors. Then there are instances when I just want to work with a particular color, and I select other colors to go with it.

Whatever method I choose, I usually select more fabrics than I will ultimately use. This allows me to "pick and choose" from my selection as I work, and I can always add still more fabrics later.

Value

Value—the lightness or darkness of a color—is very important in quilt design. This is especially true of Storm at Sea quilts, where value can dramatically change the effect of the design. To capture the movement of the Storm at Sea design, there must be good contrast between fabrics that are next to each other; otherwise the colors will blend, and the movement you want to create will be lost.

I learned an important quiltmaking lesson in a design class taught by Judi Warren. She had us arrange our fabrics into groups by value, with light values in one group, mediums in another, and darks in another. This taught me to look at fabric with any eye to value or contrast rather than color. It was a "valuable" experience. Now, after I make my initial color selection for a quilt, I group the fabrics into light, medium, and dark values. If necessary, I add light-medium and medium-dark groups as well.

Study the quilts in this book to see how value placement makes each one different. My best advice is to trust your instincts as you work. If a particular combination doesn't work as well as you expected, make changes until you are satisfied.

I often make changes as I work on a quilt, but there is a down side to doing so. With the techniques in this book, you sew units together before you can see how the design is evolving. If you decide to change something, you have to discard pieced sections. This may be difficult to do at first, but I find it becomes easier with practice!

Rotary Cutting

All the quilts in this book use rotary-cutting techniques. All the cutting measurements include ¼"-wide seam allowances. Accuracy and good tools are important. A rotary cutter, a cutting mat, and an acrylic ruler marked in ⅛" increments are essential.

When using a rotary cutter, always cut away from yourself. Hold the ruler down firmly and push the cutter along the edge of the ruler, making a firm, clean cut from edge to edge.

Straight-Cut Strips

1. Fold the fabric selvage to selvage. Make sure the selvages are aligned and perfectly parallel. Keep the folded edge smooth and even. Fold the fabric once more. You should have 4 layers of fabric.

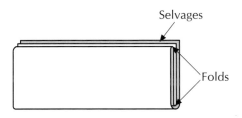

Selvages

Folds

2. Position the fabric on your cutting mat. If you have a mat with grid lines, line up the folded edge of the fabric with one of the horizontal grid lines on your mat, about 3" from the bottom edge.

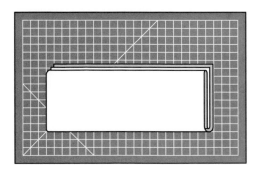

Hint

If your cutting mat does not have grid lines, you can draw two lines on it with a permanent-ink pen. The horizontal line should be 3" up from the bottom edge. The vertical line should be 3" in from the left edge (right edge for left-handed people).

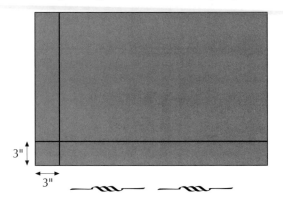

3"

3"

3. To make perpendicular cuts, place the ruler on one of the vertical grid lines (or the vertical line you have drawn). Right-handed people should position the ruler on the left edge of the fabric. Left-handed people should position the ruler on the right. Your ruler must be perfectly perpendicular to the folds or your strips will have a bend at each fold. Begin cutting by eliminating the uneven edge of the fabric. Place your ruler on top of the uneven edge and trim it away.

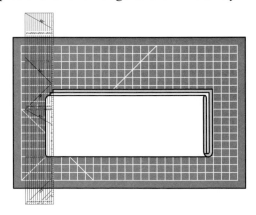

4. Use the markings on your ruler to cut strips to the appropriate width. Position the proper measurement line on the cut edge of the fabric and cut the required number of strips. The directions for each quilt will tell you how wide to cut the strips and how many to cut.

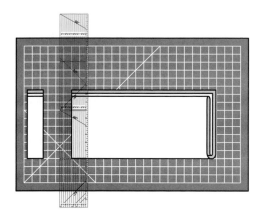

Squares

1. Cut the fabric into strips of the required width.

2. Use your ruler and rotary cutter to cut the strips into squares.

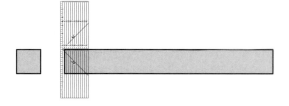

Rectangles

1. Cut the fabric into strips of the required width.

2. Use your ruler and rotary cutter to cut the strips into rectangles of the required length. (You may have to use the long edge of the ruler.)

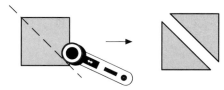

Triangles

1. Cut the fabric into strips of the required width.

2. Use your ruler and rotary cutter to cut the strips into squares.

3. Cut the squares diagonally, from corner to corner. Each square will yield 2 triangles.

Storm at Sea Units

Traditional Storm at Sea quilts are made up of units rather than blocks. In some quilts in this book, units are sewn into blocks. The following units are used:

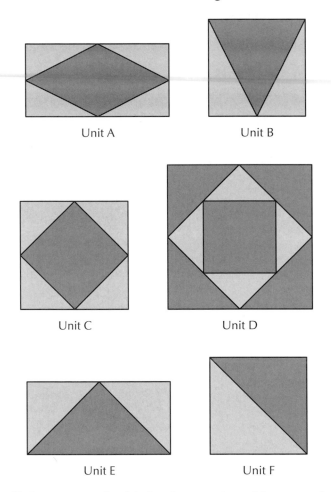

Unit A   Unit B

Unit C   Unit D

Unit E   Unit F

All the patterns in this book use a ¼"-wide seam allowance unless otherwise indicated. An accurate ¼"-wide seam allowance is extremely important. If your seam allowances are not accurate, units may not fit together correctly.

Making Unit A

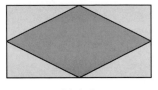

Unit A

To make each Unit A, you need 4 squares and 1 rectangle. Cut the rectangle the finished unit size plus ½" for seam allowances. Cut the squares the same size as the short sides of the cut rectangle. The rectangle will become the center diamond shape and the squares will become the elongated triangles surrounding it.

1. On the wrong sides of 2 of the squares, measure in ½ the cut width of the square plus ⅛" along the bottom right edge. Mark this point. Measure in ⅛" along the top right edge and mark. Draw a line to connect the marks. It is important that you measure and mark accurately, since this is the stitching line.

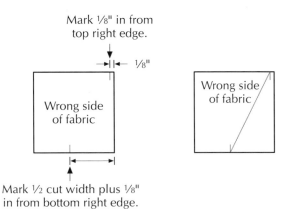

Mark ⅛" in from top right edge.

⅛"

Wrong side of fabric

Wrong side of fabric

Mark ½ cut width plus ⅛" in from bottom right edge.

2. Place a marked square on the bottom half of the rectangle, right sides together, with the wider marking on the bottom edge and the marked angle on the right side as shown. Make sure the bottom and side edges match the edges of the rectangle. Stitch on the marked line.

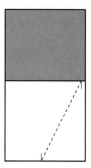

3. Place the second marked square on the top half of the rectangle, right sides together, with the wider marking on the top edge and the marked angle on the left side as shown. When you add the second marked square, flip the corner of the sewn square out of the way. Stitch on the marked line.

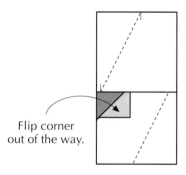

Flip corner
out of the way.

4. Press the squares outward. Trim the squares even with the rectangle and trim the seam allowances of the bottom 2 layers only to ¼".

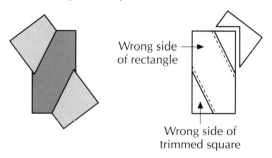

Wrong side of rectangle

Wrong side of
trimmed square

Partially completed
Unit A

Note

Squares marked from the right side are always stitched to the bottom right side and top left side of the rectangle.

5. On the wrong sides of the 2 remaining squares, measure in ½ the cut width of the square plus ⅛" along the bottom left edge. Mark this point. Measure in ⅛" along the top left edge and mark. Draw a line to connect the marks.

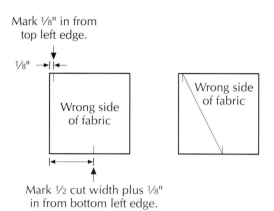

Mark ⅛" in from
top left edge.

⅛"

Wrong side
of fabric

Wrong side
of fabric

Mark ½ cut width plus ⅛"
in from bottom left edge.

6. Place 1 of the marked squares on the bottom half of the partially completed rectangle, right sides together, with the wider marking on the bottom edge and the marked angle on the left side. Stitch on the marked line.

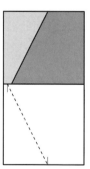

7. Place the remaining marked square on the top half of the partially completed rectangle, right sides together, with the wider marking on the top edge and the marked angle on the right side. Flip the corner of the sewn square out of the way when you add the second marked square. Stitch on the marked line.

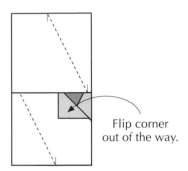

Flip corner
out of the way.

8. Press the squares outward. Trim the squares even with the rectangle and trim the seam allowances to ¼" as in step 4.

Note
Squares marked from the left side are always stitched to the bottom left side and the top right side of the rectangle.

Making Partial A Units

Some quilts include partial A units. These partial A units require only 2 squares and 1 rectangle.

To make the partial A unit below, mark and stitch the unit as shown in "Making Unit A" on pages 8–10. Use 1 square marked from the left and 1 square marked from the right. Stitch squares to the bottom of the rectangle only. It doesn't matter which square you attach first.

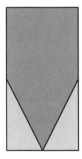

Partial Unit A

To make the partial A unit below, mark and stitch the unit as shown in "Making Unit A" on pages 8–10. Follow steps 1–4 for squares marked from the right or steps 5–8 for squares marked from the left.

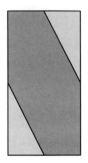

Variations of Partial Unit A

Making Unit B

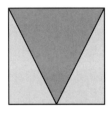

Unit B

Unit B is made from 3 squares, all the same size. One square will become the center triangle and the other 2 will form the points. Mark and stitch them as you would for Unit A.

1. On the wrong side of one of the 2 squares that will form the points, measure in ½ the cut width of the square plus ⅛" along the bottom right edge. Mark this point. Measure in ⅛" from the top right edge and mark. Draw a line to connect the marks.

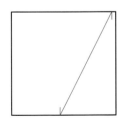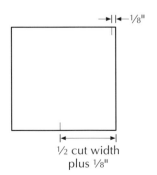

→||←—⅛"

½ cut width
plus ⅛"

2. Place the marked square on top of the center square, right sides together, with the wider marking on the bottom edge and the marked angle on the right side. Stitch on the marked line. Press the marked square outward. Trim the marked square even with the center square and trim the seam allowances of the bottom 2 layers only to ¼".

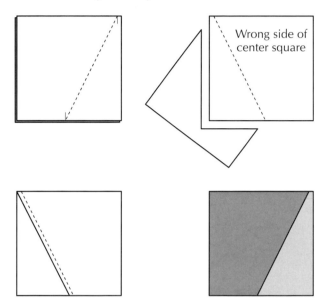

3. On the wrong side of the second square that will form the point, measure in ½ the cut width of the square plus ⅛" along the bottom left edge. Mark this point. Measure in ⅛" from the top left edge and mark. Draw a line to connect the marks.

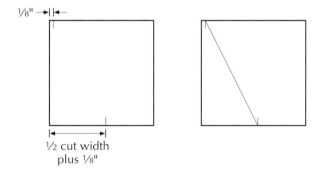

⅛" →‖←

½ cut width
plus ⅛"

4. Place the second marked square on top of the partially completed unit, right sides together, with the wider marking on the bottom edge and the marked angle on the left side. Stitch on the marked line. Press

the marked square outward. Trim the marked square even with the center square and trim the seam allowances of the bottom 2 layers only to ¼", as in step 2.

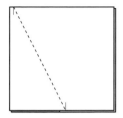

Making Unit C

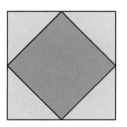

Unit C

To make this unit, use 1 large square for the center and 4 smaller squares for the corner triangles. Cut the small squares to half the finished size of the unit plus ½" for seam allowances.

1. Mark a diagonal line on the wrong side of each small square.

2. Place 2 of the marked squares on opposite corners of the large square with right sides together as shown. Stitch on the marked lines.

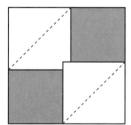

3. Trim each corner square as shown, leaving a ¼"-wide seam allowance. Do not trim the center square. Press the corner squares outward.

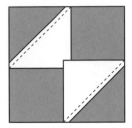 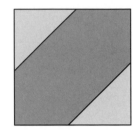

4. Stitch the remaining marked squares to the other 2 corners of the large square in the same manner. Trim and press as in step 3.

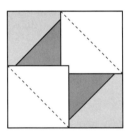

Making Partial C Units

Make partial C units in the same manner as Unit C, using just 1, 2, or 3 corner squares.

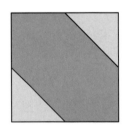 

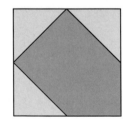

Variations of Partial Unit C

Making Unit D

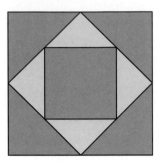

Unit D

To make this unit, add 4 triangles to a completed Unit C. Cut squares the finished size of Unit C plus ⅞" for seam allowances. Cut diagonally to make triangles.

1. Place 2 triangles on opposite sides of the unit and stitch. Press the seam allowances toward the triangles.

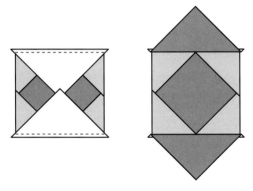

2. Stitch the remaining triangles to the other 2 sides in the same manner. Press.

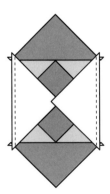

Making Unit E

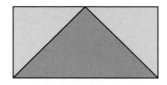

Unit E

To make this unit, use 1 rectangle and 2 squares. The rectangle will become the large center triangle and the squares will become the corner triangles.

1. Mark a diagonal line on the wrong side of each fabric square.

2. Place a marked square on 1 end of the rectangle with right sides together as shown. Stitch on the marked line.

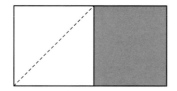

Stitch corner to corner.

3. Trim the marked square as shown, leaving a ¼"-wide seam allowance. Do not trim the rectangle. Press the corner square outward.

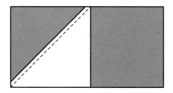

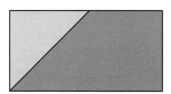

4. Stitch the remaining marked square to the other end of the rectangle in the same manner. Trim and press as in step 3.

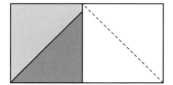

Making Unit F

Unit F

To make this unit, use squares of 2 different fabrics. Each pair of squares yields 2 units.

1. From each fabric, cut the required number of strips ⅞" larger than the finished measurement of the unit. If your finished unit will measure 2" x 2", cut strips 2⅞" wide.

2. Crosscut the strips into squares.

3. Pick up 1 square of each fabric. Mark a diagonal line on the wrong side of the lighter square.

4. Place squares right sides together with the marked square on top. Stitch ¼" from the line on either side.

Hint
If the edge of your presser foot is not exactly ¼" from the needle, try shifting the needle position. If this doesn't work, you might need to mark the seam line.

5. Cut apart on the marked center line, open, and press the seam allowances toward the darker fabric. Trim the points from the corners as shown.

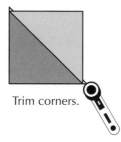

Trim corners.

Squaring Up

No matter how carefully I cut and stitch, pieced units and blocks sometimes end up with uneven edges. I always take the time to check measurements and square up blocks if necessary.

It is surprising what a difference squaring up can make. Even though you are just trimming away slivers of fabric, squaring up makes the units or blocks neater and uniformly sized. I find it's worth the extra effort.

1. Place your ruler on the completed unit or block. Line up one of the lines on the ruler with either the center of the unit (point to point) or a convenient seam, as shown. Measure from that line, making sure you still have a ¼"-wide seam allowance at the outside edge. Use a rotary cutter to trim away excess fabric.

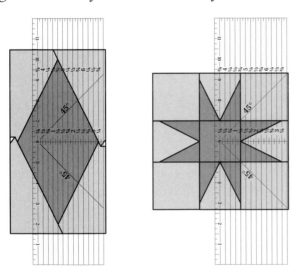

2. Repeat for all 4 sides of the unit or block.

Assembling the Units

The points in Storm at Sea designs need to match exactly, so you must pin units before sewing them together. Insert a pin through the points where the seam lines should meet, and match and pin the outside edges. Stitch with ¼"-wide seams, stitching across the top of the point.

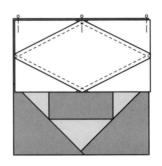
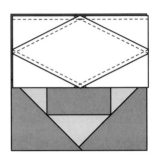

Hint

If you need to ease in fullness when joining blocks, pull the block edge gently and ease in the excess as you stitch. If one edge is considerably longer than the other, pin the units as described above, inserting pins in opposite directions to ease in fullness. The more fullness there is, the more pins you need to use. Stitch with the shorter piece on top.

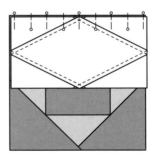

Pressing

The traditional rule in quiltmaking is to press the seam allowances in one direction. In Storm at Sea quilts, many seams come together at one point. Pressing to one side adds bulk. The best way to handle this is to press the seams open between units. The units will lie flat and the points will be smooth.

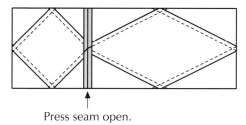

Press seam open.

Assembling the Quilt Top

Once you've made all the units or blocks for a quilt, stitch them together. One way to do this is to sew the blocks into rows, then join the rows.

The method I use most often is to stitch the units into pairs, then join the pairs, and so on. I continue joining units this way until I've assembled the entire quilt top. This method eliminates the need to stitch long rows together and makes joining units easier.

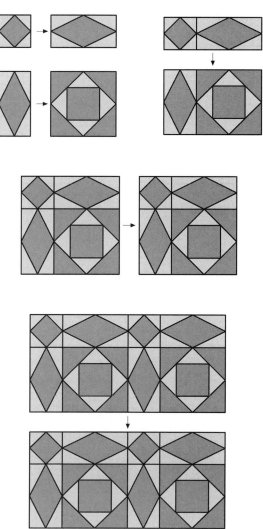

Designing Storm at Sea Quilts

I have included a Storm at Sea grid (page 79) so that you can create your own designs. Either trace the grid or make photocopies. You could also use a computer and one of the many quilt-design programs available. Play with the design, and consider changing the grid by eliminating lines or sections.

I like to start by working with value alone—no color. This allows me to see and explore design possibilities instead of getting caught up in color choices. Use a black marker for the dark values and a pencil for the medium values. Leave the paper unmarked for the light values. Use changes in value to emphasize movement in your design.

Once you have a design you like, rework it with colored pencils. Explore color options and consider possible fabrics.

Sometimes it takes several attempts to create a design that you like. Don't be dismayed. I designed many of the quilts in this book by trial and error. An idea that does not work is often the inspiration for one that does.

I encourage you to take time to play. Experimenting is a lot of fun; it broadens your horizons and gives you a chance to act like a kid again. Enjoy yourself and Quilt Up a Storm!

Flotsam and Jetsam
by Lydia Quigley, 1993, Kingston, Ontario, Canada, 48½" x 56"
Cool blues and greens combine with hot pinks to update the classic Storm at Sea design.
Directions begin on page 29.

Sewing Up a Storm

by Lydia Quigley, 1993, Kingston, Ontario, Canada, 41½" x 41½"
The dark needle-and-thread fabric is the perfect background for this appropriately named Storm at Sea design. Directions begin on page 35.

Tropical Punch
by Lydia Quigley, 1993, Kingston, Ontario, Canada, 37½" x 37½"
A floral print sets the color scheme for this bright and cheerful Storm at Sea design.
Directions begin on page 38.

Heart Throb

by Lydia Quigley, 1993, Kingston, Ontario, Canada, 37½" x 55"
Many pink and red fabrics are combined in this unique Storm at Sea design. Directions begin on page 41.

Floral Fanta-Sea

by Lydia Quigley, 1993, Kingston, Ontario, Canada, 69½" x 69½"

Soft florals set the theme for this adaptation of the Storm at Sea design. Quilted by Pam MacGregor.
Directions begin on page 48.

Regatta

by Lydia Quigley, 1993, Kingston, Ontario, Canada, 38½" x 46"

Colorful sailboats skim across the surface of the sea. A most appropriate adaptation of the Storm at Sea design. Directions begin on page 52.

Dream Weaver

by Lydia Quigley, 1993, Kingston, Ontario, Canada, 35" x 42½"
A variety of colors weave across the surface of this exciting Storm at Sea design.
Directions begin on page 58.

Surrounded Stars

by Lydia Quigley, 1993, Kingston, Ontario, Canada, 53½" x 65½"
The floral border of this lovely quilt sets the color scheme for the stars and surrounding lattice.
Directions begin on page 45.

Field of Flowers

by Lydia Quigley, 1993, Kingston, Ontario, Canada, 43¾" x 55"

Bright, cheerful flowers bloom in profusion in this eye-catching quilt. Directions begin on page 62.

School of Fish

by Lydia Quigley, 1993, Kingston, Ontario, Canada, 44½" x 53"
Tropical fish swim in the depths of the sea in this unique, colorful quilt. Directions begin on page 70.

Aquarius
by Lydia Quigley, 1993, Kingston, Ontario, Canada, 78" x 78"
A wide variety of fabrics and subtle shading create a feeling of depth and motion in this wonderful quilt.
Directions begin on page 67.

Stars at Sea

**by Lydia Quigley, 1989,
Kingston, Ontario, Canada,
36½" x 36½"**

*Fabrics that shade from light to
dark give this Storm at Sea
design a traditional look.*
Directions begin on page 32.

Stars at Sea II

**by Lydia Quigley, 1990,
Kingston, Ontario, Canada,
36½" x 36½"**

*Bold colors and fabrics create
a completely different
"Stars at Sea."*
Directions begin on page 32.

Flotsam and Jetsam

Finished Size: 48½" x 56"
Finished Unit A Size: 5" x 2½"
Finished Unit C Size: 2½" x 2½"
Finished Unit D Size: 5" x 5"

Color Photo: Page 17

You can make a great scrap quilt with the Storm at Sea design. For "Flotsam and Jetsam," I combined a light multicolored print with a wide variety of blue, green, and pink prints. The pink area that extends across the surface of the quilt adds a warm glow of contrast against the coolness of the blues and greens.

Fabric Key

Light

Assorted mediums

Dark pink

Blue

Materials: 44"-wide fabric

2¾ yds. light print

2¼ yds. total assorted medium prints in shades of blue, green, and pink

⅓ yd. dark pink print for inner border

1 yd. blue print for outer border and binding

2⅞ yds. for backing

Cutting Chart

FABRIC	FIRST CUT		SECOND CUT	
	No. of Strips	Strip Width	No. of Pieces	Dimensions
Light Print	7	2¼"	120	2¼" x 2¼"
	24	3"	326	3" x 3"
Medium Prints	3 total	4"	30	4" x 4"
	5 total	3⅜"	60	3⅜" x 3⅜"
	11 total	3"	71	3" x 5½"
	7 total	1¾"	168	1¾" x 1¾"
Dark Pink	5	1½" (INNER BORDER)		
Blue	5	3½" (OUTER BORDER)		
	6	2" (BINDING)		

Storm at Sea Units

To make each unit, refer to the fabric key on page 29 and the illustrations that follow.

Unit A

1. Mark a sewing line on wrong side of the following 3" light squares.

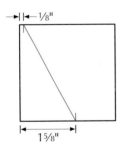

Mark 142 from the left-hand edge.   Mark 142 from the right-hand edge.

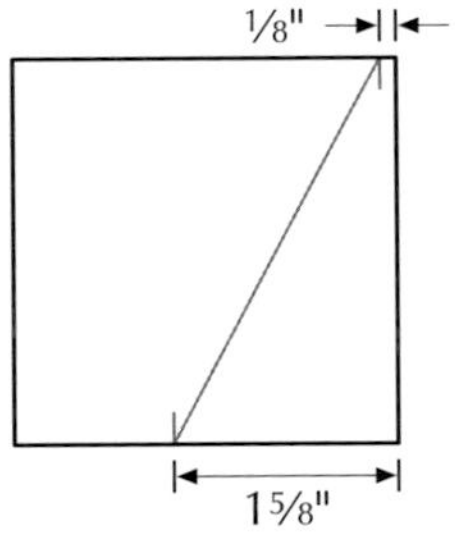

2. Following the directions on pages 8–10, piece A units using the 3" x 5½" medium rectangles and the marked 3" light squares. Make 12 A units with pink rectangles.

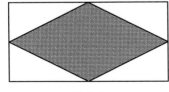

Unit A
Make 71.

Unit C

Following the directions on pages 11–12, piece C units using the 42 remaining 3" light squares for the centers and the 1¾" medium squares for the corners. Make 7 C units with mostly pink 1¾" squares.

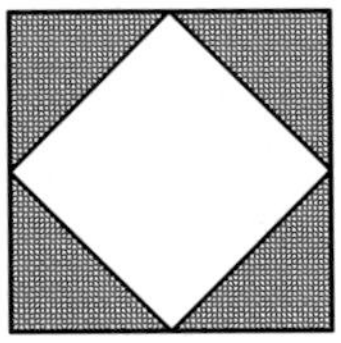

Unit C
Make 42.

Unit D

1. Cut the 3⅜" medium squares in half diagonally. You will have 120 triangles.

2. Following the directions on page 12, piece D units using the 4" medium squares, the 2¼" light squares, and the medium triangles from step 1. Make 8 D units with mostly pink 4" squares and triangles.

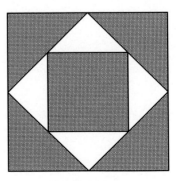

Unit D
Make 30.

Quilt Top Assembly

Arrange the completed units so that you have an area of mostly pink units. Refer to the color photo on page 17. This pink area does not have to match the photograph exactly; it can flow randomly in any direction across the surface of the quilt.

Stitch the units together, referring to "Assembling the Quilt Top" on page 15. Press the joining seams open.

Borders

Refer to pages 74–76.

1. Measure, cut, mark, and attach 1½"-wide pink inner borders to the quilt top, piecing strips as needed.

2. Add the 3½"-wide blue outer borders to the quilt in the same way.

Quilt Finishing

Refer to pages 76–78.

1. Layer the quilt top with batting and backing; baste.

2. Quilt a design of your choice or quilt in-the-ditch.

3. Piece binding strips together and bind quilt edges.

Stars at Sea

An ivory-and-blue color scheme gives this Storm at Sea design a traditional look. Bolder fabrics and a different color scheme can change the same design dramatically (see "Stars at Sea II" on page 28).

__Finished Size: 36½" x 36½"__
Finished Unit A Size: 4" x 8"
Finished Unit B Size: 4" x 4"
Finished Unit C Size: 4" x 4"
Finished Unit D Size: 8" x 8"

Color Photo: Page 28

Fabric Key

Dark navy blue

Medium navy blue

Medium blue

Ivory-and-blue

Ivory

Materials: 44"-wide fabric

¼ yd. dark navy blue print (dark value)

1⅜ yds. medium navy blue print for blocks and binding (medium-dark value)

½ yd. medium blue print (medium value)

¾ yd. ivory-and-blue print (light-medium value)

1 yd. ivory print (light value)

1⅛ yds. for backing

Cutting Chart

FABRIC	FIRST CUT		SECOND CUT	
	NO. OF STRIPS	STRIP WIDTH	NO. OF PIECES	DIMENSIONS
DARK NAVY BLUE	1	4½"	4	4½" x 8½"
			4	2½" x 2½"
MEDIUM NAVY BLUE			2	4⅞" x 4⅞"
	6	4½"	12	4½" x 4½"
			8	4½" x 8½"
			4	4½" x 20½"
	1	2½"	16	2½" x 2½"
	4	2" (BINDING)		
MEDIUM BLUE	1	4⅞"	6	4⅞" x 4⅞"
			1	4½" x 4½"
	1	2½"	16	2½" x 2½"
IVORY-AND-BLUE	1	6¼"	4	6¼" x 6¼"
	4	4½"	32	4½" x 4½"
IVORY	5	4½"	40	4½" x 4½"
	2	3⅜"	16	3⅜" x 3⅜"

Storm at Sea Units

To make each unit, refer to the fabric key on page 32 and the illustrations that follow.

Unit A

1. Mark a sewing line on wrong side of the following 4½" squares.

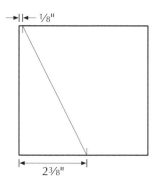

Mark from the left-hand edge:
20 ivory
12 ivory-and-blue

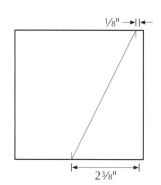

Mark from the right-hand edge:
20 ivory
12 ivory-and-blue

2. Following the directions on pages 8–10, piece A units. Make Unit A in 2 color schemes as shown above right. Use 4½" x 8½" medium navy blue and dark navy blue rectangles and marked 4½" ivory-and-blue and ivory squares. You will have 16 ivory squares left over for Unit B.

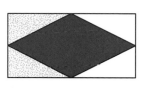

Unit A
Make 4.

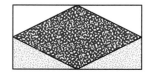

Unit A
Make 8.

Unit B

Following the directions on pages 10–11, piece B units using 4½" medium navy blue squares and the remaining marked 4½" ivory squares. You will have 4 medium navy blue squares left over for the border.

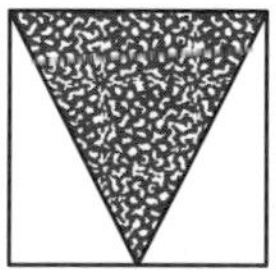

Unit B
Make 8.

Unit C

Following the directions on pages 11–12, piece C units. Make Unit C in 3 color schemes. Use 4½" squares for centers and 2½" squares for corners.

Unit C
Make 1.

Unit C
Make 4.

Unit C
Make 4.

Unit D

1. Cut the 4⅞" medium navy blue and medium blue squares in half diagonally. You will have a total of 16 triangles.

2. Following the directions on page 12, piece D units using the 6¼" ivory-and-blue squares, the 3⅜" ivory squares, and the triangles from step 1.

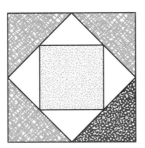

Unit D
Make 4.

Quilt Top Assembly

Arrange the completed A, C, and D units following the quilt plan. Stitch the units together, referring to "Assembling the Quilt Top" on page 15. Press the joining seams open.

Borders

1. Stitch a Unit B to each end of the 4½" x 20½" medium navy blue strips as shown. Press seams open.

Make 4.

2. Stitch one of the resulting units to each side of the quilt top, referring to the diagram on page 32 for placement. Press.

3. For top and bottom borders, add a 4½" medium navy blue square to each end of the remaining border units as shown. Press seams open.

Make 2.

4. Stitch top and bottom borders to quilt top. Press.

Quilt Finishing

Refer to pages 76–78.

1. Layer the quilt top with batting and backing; baste.

2. Quilt a design of your choice.

3. Piece binding strips together and bind quilt edges.

Sewing Up a Storm

This design is similar to "Stars at Sea" on page 32. Just change the color and value placement, add an extra unit, and a new design emerges.

Finished Size: 41½" x 41½"
Finished Unit A Size: 4" x 8"
Finished Unit B Size: 4" x 4"
Finished Unit C Size: 4" x 4"
Finished Unit D Size: 8" x 8"
Finished Unit E Size: 4" x 8"

Color Photo: Page 18

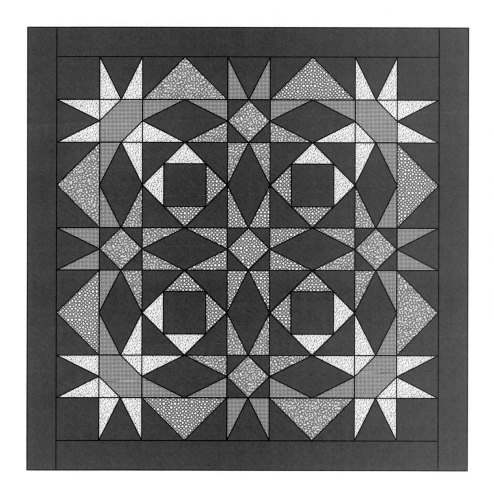

Fabric Key

Black

Gold

Bright green

Bright blue

Bright pink

Materials: 44"-wide fabric

1⅞ yds. black print for
  background and border
¾ yd. gold
⅔ yd. bright green

⅔ yd. bright blue
½ yd. bright pink
1½ yds. for backing

Cutting Chart

FABRIC	FIRST CUT		SECOND CUT	
	NO. OF STRIPS	STRIP WIDTH	NO. OF PIECES	DIMENSIONS
BLACK	1	6¼"	4	6¼" x 6¼"
	1	4⅞"	8	4⅞" x 4⅞"
	7	4½"	32	4½" x 4½"
			12	4½" x 8½"
	2	2½"	20	2½" x 2½"
	4	3" (BORDER)		
GOLD	3	4½"	24	4½" x 4½"
	1	3⅜"	8	3⅜" x 3⅜"
	1	2½"	8	2½" x 2½"
	1	2" (BINDING)		
BRIGHT GREEN	4	4½"	20	4½" x 4½"
			4	4½" x 8½"
	1	2" (BINDING)		
BRIGHT BLUE	4	4½"	28	4½" x 4½"
	1	2" (BINDING)		
BRIGHT PINK	2	4½"	9	4½" x 4½"
			4	4½" x 8½"
	1	3⅜"	8	3⅜" x 3⅜"
	1	2" (BINDING)		

Storm at Sea Units

To make each unit, refer to the fabric key on page 35 and the illustrations that follow.

Unit A

1. Mark a sewing line on wrong side of the following 4½" squares.

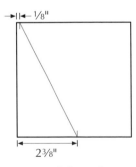

2⅜"

**Mark from the
left-hand edge:**
4 bright pink
8 bright green
12 bright blue
12 gold

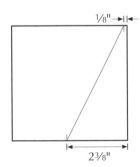

2⅜"

**Mark from the
right-hand edge:**
4 bright pink
8 bright green
12 bright blue
12 gold

2. Following the directions on pages 8–10, piece A units. Make Unit A in 3 color schemes. Use 4½" x 8½" black rectangles and marked 4½" bright squares.

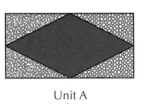

Unit A
Make 4.

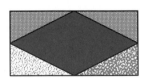

Unit A
Make 4.

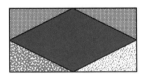

Unit A
Make 4.

Unit B

Following the directions on pages 10–11, piece B units. Make Unit B in 2 color schemes. For both variations, use 4½" black squares and marked 4½" bright squares.

Unit B
Make 8.

Unit B
Make 4.

Unit C and Partial Unit C

Piece C units, following directions on pages 11–12. Make Unit C in 3 color schemes. For C units, use 4½" squares for centers and 2½" squares for corners.

Unit C
Make 4.

Unit C
Make 1.

Partial Unit C
Make 4.

Unit D

1. Cut the 4⅞" black squares in half diagonally. You will have 16 triangles.

2. Piece D units, following the directions on page 12. Use the 6¼" black squares, the 3⅜" squares, and the triangles from step 1.

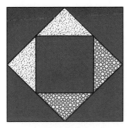

Unit D
Make 4.

Unit E

Following the directions on page 13, piece E units. Make Unit E in 2 color schemes. For all E units, use 4½" x 8½" bright rectangles and 4½" black squares.

Unit E
Make 4.

Unit E
Make 4.

Quilt Top Assembly

Arrange the completed units following the quilt plan. Stitch the units together, referring to "Assembling the Quilt Top" on page 15. Press the joining seams open.

Borders

Refer to pages 74–76.

Measure, cut, mark, and attach the 3"-wide black borders to the quilt top.

Quilt Finishing

Refer to pages 76–78.

1. To piece the backing, cut 2 crosswise strips, each 3½" wide, from your backing fabric. Join the strips end to end and attach to one long edge of the fabric as shown. Press the seams open.

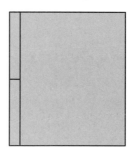

2. Layer the quilt top with batting and backing; baste.

3. Quilt a design of your choice.

4. Cut the 2"-wide binding strips into various lengths. Piece with diagonal seams to make 1 strip, approximately 180" long. (Cut additional strips from your leftover fabric if necessary.) Bind the quilt edges.

Tropical Punch

A traditional Storm at Sea design, a simple piecing variation, and bright tropical colors make this quilt a knockout.

Finished Size: *37½" x 37½"*
Finished Unit A Size: 3" x 6"
Finished Unit C Sizes:
3" x 3" and 6" x 6"
Finished Unit D Size: 6" x 6"

Color Photo: Page 19

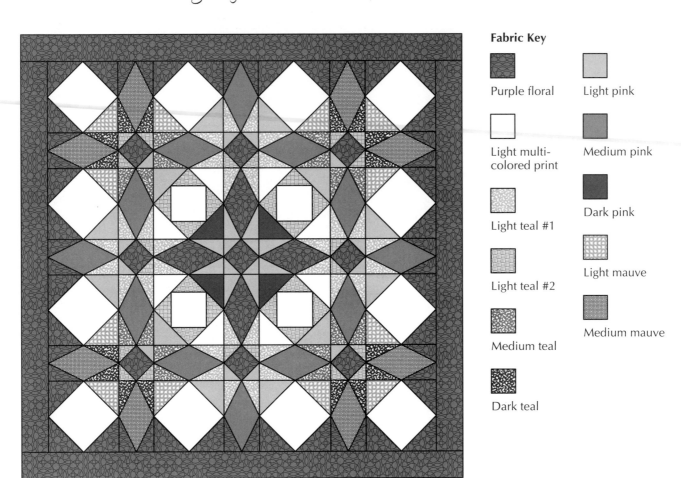

Fabric Key

Purple floral

Light pink

Light multi-colored print

Medium pink

Light teal #1

Dark pink

Light teal #2

Light mauve

Medium teal

Medium mauve

Dark teal

Materials: 44"-wide fabric

1¼ yds. purple floral print for blocks, border, and binding
¾ yd. light multicolored print
⅜ yd. light teal print #1 (low contrast)
¼ yd. light teal print #2 (high contrast)
¼ yd. medium teal print

¼ yd. dark teal print
½ yd. light pink print
¼ yd. medium pink print
¼ yd. dark pink print (or a scrap, at least 5" x 10")
⅛ yd. light mauve print
¼ yd. medium mauve print
1⅛ yds. for backing

Cutting Chart

FABRIC	FIRST CUT		SECOND CUT	
	No. of Strips	Strip Width	No. of Pieces	Dimensions
PURPLE FLORAL	6	3½"	61	3½" x 3½"
			4	3½" x 6½"
	4	2½" (BORDER)		
	4	2" (BINDING)		
LIGHT MULTICOLORED	2	6½"	12	6½" x 6½"
	1	4¾"	4	4¾" x 4¾"
	1	3⅞"	4	3⅞" x 3⅞"
LIGHT TEAL #1	3	3½"	32	3½" x 3½"
LIGHT TEAL #2	1	2⅝"	16	2⅝" x 2⅝"
	1	2"	20	2" x 2"
MEDIUM TEAL	2	3½"	16	3½" x 3½"
DARK TEAL	2	3½"	16	3½" x 3½"
LIGHT PINK			2	3⅞" x 3⅞"
	2	3½"	16	3½" x 3½"
	1	2"	16	2" x 2"
MEDIUM PINK	2	3½"	12	3½" x 6½"
DARK PINK			2	3⅞" x 3⅞"
LIGHT MAUVE	1	3½"	12	3½" x 3½"
MEDIUM MAUVE	2	3½"	8	3½" x 6½"

Storm at Sea Units

To make each unit, refer to the fabric key on page 38 and the illustrations that follow.

Unit A

1. Mark a sewing line on wrong side of the following 3½" squares.

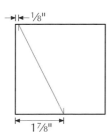

Mark from the
left-hand edge:
12 purple floral
4 light pink
16 light teal #1
8 medium teal
8 dark teal

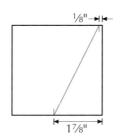

Mark from the
right-hand edge:
12 purple floral
4 light pink
16 light teal #1
8 medium teal
8 dark teal

2. Following the directions on pages 8–10, piece A units. Make Unit A in 4 color schemes. All A units use 3½" x 6½" rectangles and marked 3½" squares.

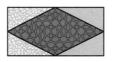

Unit A
Make 4.

Unit A
Make 8.

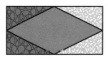

Unit A
Make 4.

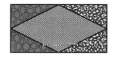

Unit A
Make 8.

Unit C

Following the directions on pages 11–12, piece C units. Make Unit C in 2 sizes. Make each size in 3 color schemes. For the small C units, use 3½" floral squares for the centers and 2" squares for the corners. For the large C units, use 6½" multicolored squares for the centers and the remaining 3½" squares for corners.

Small Unit C
Make 1.

Small Unit C
Make 4.

Small Unit C
Make 4.

Large Unit C
Make 4.

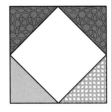
Large Unit C
Make 4.

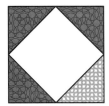
Large Unit C
Make 4.

Unit D

1. Cut the 3⅞" light pink, dark pink, and multicolored squares in half diagonally. You will have a total of 16 triangles.

2. Following the directions on page 12, piece D units using the 4¾" multicolored squares, the 2⅝" teal #2 squares, and the triangles from step 1.

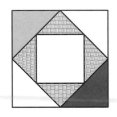
Unit D
Make 4.

Quilt Top Assembly

Arrange the completed units following the quilt plan. Stitch the units together, referring to "Assembling the Quilt Top" on page 15. Press the joining seams open.

Borders

Refer to pages 74–76.

Measure, cut, mark, and attach the 2½"-wide floral borders to the quilt top.

Quilt Finishing

Refer to pages 76–78.

1. Layer the quilt top with batting and backing; baste.

2. Quilt a design of your choice.

3. Piece binding strips together and bind quilt edges.

Heart Throb

Finished Size: 37½" x 55"
Finished Unit A Size: 3½" x 7"
Finished Unit C Size: 3½" x 3½"
Finished Unit D Size: 7" x 7"

Color Photo: Page 20

The Storm at Sea pattern lends itself to all kinds of unexpected variations.
The variety of pink and red prints makes "Heart Throb" special.

Fabric Key

☐ Assorted lights

▨ Assorted pinks

▨ Assorted reds

■ Assorted dark reds

▨ Floral

Materials: 44"-wide fabric

1⅓ yds. *total* assorted light prints
1 yd. *total* assorted pink prints
1 yd. *total* assorted red prints
1 yd. *total* assorted dark red prints

¼ yd. dark red print for inner border
1⅛ yds. pink floral print for outer border and binding
1⅝ yds. for backing

Cutting Chart

FABRIC	CUT	
	NO. OF PIECES	DIMENSIONS
ASSORTED	2	5½" x 5½"
LIGHTS	3	4⅜" x 4⅜"
	2	4" x 7½"
	37	4" x 4"
	8	3" x 3"
	12	2" x 7½"
	14	2" x 4"
	4	2" x 2"
ASSORTED	2	5½" x 5½"
PINKS	4	4⅜" x 4⅜"
	5	4" x 7½"
	17	4" x 4"
	8	3" x 3"
	8	2¼" x 2¼"
ASSORTED	2	5½" x 5½"
REDS	4	4⅜" x 4⅜"
	5	4" x 7½"
	17	4" x 4"
	8	3" x 3"
	8	2¼" x 2¼"
ASSORTED	2	5½" x 5½"
DARK REDS	5	4⅜" x 4⅜"
	8	4" x 7½"
	21	4" x 4"
	8	3" x 3"
	10	2¼" x 2¼"
DARK RED FOR BORDER	5	1¼" x 42" (INNER BORDER)
PINK	5	4½" x 42" (OUTER BORDER)
FLORAL	5	2" x 42" (BINDING)

Storm at Sea Units

To make each unit, refer to the fabric key on page 41 and the illustrations that follow.

Unit A

1. Mark a sewing line on wrong side of the following 4" squares.

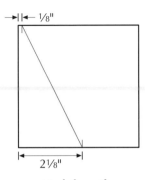 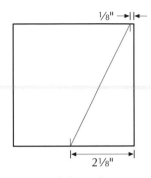

Mark from the left-hand edge:
14 assorted lights
8 assorted pinks
8 assorted reds
10 assorted dark reds

Mark from the right-hand edge:
14 assorted lights
8 assorted pinks
8 assorted reds
10 assorted dark reds

2. Following the directions on pages 8–10, piece A units. Make Unit A in 12 color schemes. For all A units, use the 4" x 7½" rectangles and the marked 4" squares.

Unit C and Partial Unit C

Following the directions on pages 11–12, piece C units and partial C units. Make Unit C in 10 color schemes and in 3 piecing variations. For all C units, use 4" squares for centers and 2¼" squares for corners.

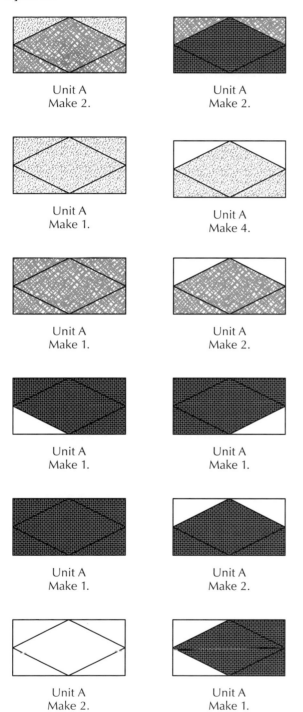

Unit A
Make 2.

Unit A
Make 2.

Unit A
Make 1.

Unit A
Make 4.

Unit A
Make 1.

Unit A
Make 2.

Unit A
Make 1.

Unit A
Make 1.

Unit A
Make 1.

Unit A
Make 2.

Unit A
Make 2.

Unit A
Make 1.

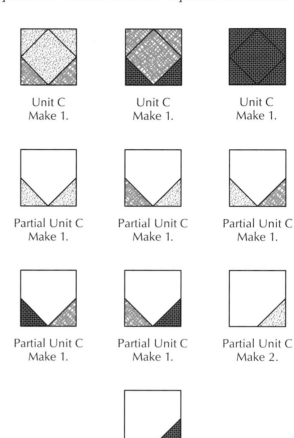

Unit C
Make 1.

Unit C
Make 1.

Unit C
Make 1.

Partial Unit C
Make 1.

Partial Unit C
Make 1.

Partial Unit C
Make 1.

Partial Unit C
Make 1.

Partial Unit C
Make 1.

Partial Unit C
Make 2.

Partial Unit C
Make 2.

Unit D

1. Cut the 4⅜" squares in half diagonally. You will have a total of 32 triangles.

2. Following the directions on page 12, piece D units. Make Unit D in 4 color schemes. For all D units, use 5½" squares, 3" squares, and triangles from step 1.

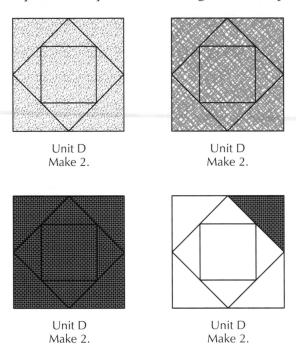

Unit D
Make 2.

Unit D
Make 2.

Unit D
Make 2.

Unit D
Make 2.

Quilt Top Assembly

Arrange the completed units and the light rectangles and squares following the quilt plan. Stitch the units together, referring to "Assembling the Quilt Top" on page 15. Press the joining seams open.

Borders

Refer to pages 74–76.

1. Measure, cut, mark, and attach 1¼" dark red inner borders to the quilt top, piecing strips as needed.

2. Add the 4½"-wide floral outer borders to the quilt in the same way.

Quilt Finishing

Refer to pages 76–78.

1. Layer the quilt top with batting and backing; baste.

2. Quilt a design of your choice.

3. Piece binding strips together and bind quilt edges.

Surrounded Stars

You can use Storm at Sea units to make many traditional quilt blocks. "Surrounded Stars" features a traditional design in an unusual setting.

Finished Size: 53½" x 65½"
Finished Unit B Size: 3" x 3"
Finished Unit C Size: 3" x 3"
Finished Unit F Size: 3" x 3"
Finished Block Size: 9" x 9"

Color Photo: Page 24

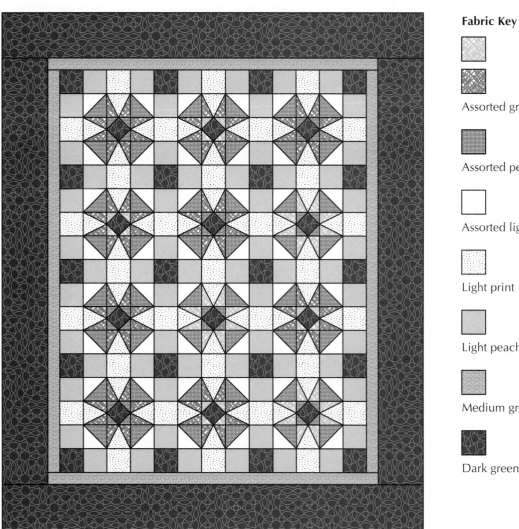

Fabric Key

Assorted greens

Assorted peaches

Assorted lights

Light print

Light peach

Medium green

Dark green floral

Materials: 44"-wide fabric

⅛ yd. *each* of 12 assorted green prints (1 yd. if using 1 fabric)

⅛ yd. or one 8" x 8" scrap *each* of 12 assorted peach prints (¾ yd. if using 1 fabric)

⅛ yd. or one 4" x 8" scrap *each* of 12 assorted light prints (½ yd. if using 1 fabric)

⅞ yd. light print for background

¾ yd. light peach print

⅜ yd. medium green print for inner border

1⅞ yds. dark green floral print for blocks, sashing squares, outer border, and binding

3¼ yds. for backing

Cutting Chart

| FABRIC | FIRST CUT | | SECOND CUT | |
	NO. OF STRIPS	STRIP WIDTH	NO. OF PIECES	DIMENSIONS
12 ASSORTED GREENS	1*	3½"	8 (96 TOTAL)	3½" x 3½"
4 LIGHTEST GREENS			4*(16 TOTAL)	2" x 2"
12 ASSORTED PEACHES			2*(24 TOTAL)	3⅞" x 3⅞"
8 ASSORTED PEACHES			4*(32 TOTAL)	2" x 2"
ASSORTED LIGHTS			2*(24 TOTAL)	3⅞" x 3⅞"
LIGHT PRINT	4	3½"	48	3½" x 3½"
	3	3½" (SASHING)		
LIGHT PEACH	6	3½" (SASHING)		
MEDIUM GREEN	5	2" (INNER BORDER)		
DARK GREEN FLORAL	3	3½"	32	3½" x 3½"
	6	6" (OUTER BORDER)		
	7	2" (BINDING)		

*FROM EACH FABRIC

Storm at Sea Units

To make each unit, refer to the fabric key on page 45 and the illustrations that follow.

Unit B

1. Mark a sewing line on the wrong side of the 3½" assorted green squares.

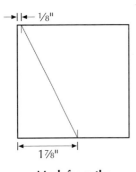 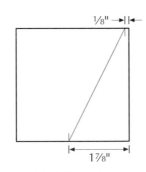

Mark from the left-hand edge:
4 from each green

Mark from the right-hand edge:
4 from each green

2. Following the directions on pages 10–11, piece B units using the 3½" light-print squares and the marked 3½" assorted green squares. Make 4 units from each green fabric.

Unit B
Make 48.

Unit C

Following the directions on pages 11–12, piece C units using 3½" dark green floral squares for the centers and the 2" assorted peach and green squares for the corners. In each unit, use the same fabric for all 4 corners. You will have 20 floral squares left over for the sashing.

Unit C
Make 4.

Unit C
Make 8.

Unit F

Following the directions on page 13, piece F units using the 3⅞" assorted peach squares and the 3⅞" assorted light squares. Pair the 2 squares from each peach fabric with 2 squares from the same light fabric for a total of 4 units from each pair of fabrics.

Unit F
Make 48.

Block Assembly

1. Arrange units as shown in the illustration below.

2. Sew units into rows, then sew rows together. Press joining seams open.

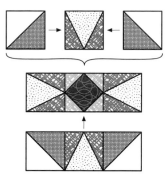

Make 12.

Sashing Units

1. Stitch a 3½" light peach strip to each side of a 3½" light print strip. Press the seam allowances toward the light peach strips.

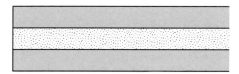

Make 3.

2. Crosscut the strip sets into a total of 31 segments, each 3½" wide.

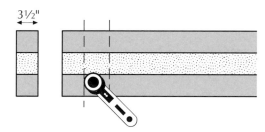

Quilt Top Assembly

1. Following the quilt plan, arrange the Star blocks, sashing units, and remaining 3½" floral squares.

2. Sew 3½" dark green floral squares and sashing units into rows as shown. Press the seam allowances toward the sashing units.

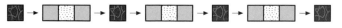

Make 5.

3. Sew sashing units and Star blocks into rows as shown. Press seam allowances toward sashing units.

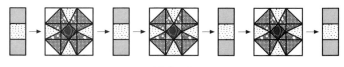

Make 4.

4. Join the rows. Press the seam allowances toward the sashing rows.

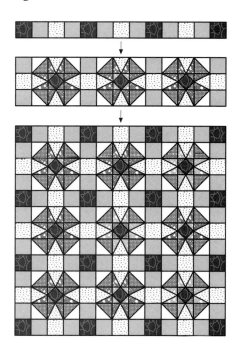

Borders

Refer to pages 74–76.

1. Measure, cut, mark, and attach 2"-wide medium green inner-border strips to the quilt top, piecing as needed.

2. Add the 6"-wide dark green floral outer borders to the quilt in the same way.

Quilt Finishing

Refer to pages 76–78.

1. Layer the quilt top with batting and backing; baste.

2. Quilt as desired.

3. Piece binding strips together and bind quilt edges.

Floral Santa-Sea

Finished Size: 69½" x 69½"
Finished Unit A Size: 3" x 6"
Finished Unit C Size: 3" x 3"
Finished Unit D Size: 6" x 6"

Color Photo: Page 21

Eliminating design lines from the traditional Storm at Sea layout created a wonderful new pattern. The quilt on page 21 uses one background fabric throughout and four colors each for flowers and leaves. This design would also be pretty with just one color for the flowers and another for the leaves.

Fabric Key

Light	Dark blue
Medium pink	Green #1
Dark pink	Green #2
Medium coral	Green #3
Dark coral	Green #4
Medium purple	Gold
Dark purple	Multicolored floral
Medium blue	

Materials: 44"-wide fabric

4 yds. light print for background
½ yd. medium pink print
⅝ yd. dark pink print
½ yd. medium coral print
½ yd. dark coral print
½ yd. medium purple print
½ yd. dark purple print
½ yd. medium blue print

½ yd. dark blue print
½ yd. green print #1
⅜ yd. *each* 3 additional green prints
¼ yd. gold print
1⅔ yds. multicolored floral for outer border and binding
4 yds. for backing

Cutting Chart

FABRIC	FIRST CUT		SECOND CUT	
	NO. OF STRIPS	STRIP WIDTH	NO. OF PIECES	DIMENSIONS
LIGHT PRINT	5	4¾"	36	4¾" x 4¾"
	5	3⅞"	46	3⅞" x 3⅞"
	20	3½"	212	3½" x 3½"
			8	3½" x 6½"
	5	2"	96	2" x 2"
	6	2" (INNER BORDER)		
MEDIUM PINK	1	3⅞"	8	3⅞" x 3⅞"
	1	3½"	3	3½" x 6½"
	2	2⅝"	32	2⅝" x 2⅝"
DARK PINK	4	3½"	32	3½" x 3½"
			3	3½" x 6½"
	1	2"	16	2" x 2"
MEDIUM CORAL	1	3⅞"	6	3⅞" x 3⅞"
	1	3½"	3	3½" x 6½"
	2	2⅝"	24	2⅝" x 2⅝"
DARK CORAL	3	3½"	24	3½" x 3½"
			3	3½" x 6½"
	1	2"	12	2" x 2"
MEDIUM PURPLE	1	3⅞"	6	3⅞" x 3⅞"
	1	3½"	3	3½" x 6½"
	2	2⅝"	24	2⅝" x 2⅝"
DARK PURPLE	3	3½"	24	3½" x 3½"
			3	3½" x 6½"
	1	2"	12	2" x 2"
MEDIUM BLUE	1	3⅞"	6	3⅞" x 3⅞"
	1	3½"	3	3½" x 6½"
	2	2⅝"	24	2⅝" x 2⅝"
DARK BLUE	3	3½"	24	3½" x 3½"
			3	3½" x 6½"
	1	2"	12	2" x 2"
GREEN #1	4	3½"	16	3½" x 6½"
			6	3½" x 3½"
3 REMAINING GREENS	3 FROM EACH FABRIC	3½"	12 (36 TOTAL)	3½" x 6½"
			6 (18 TOTAL)	3½" x 3½"
GOLD	2	3½"	13	3½" x 3½"
MULTICOLORED FLORAL	7	5" (OUTER BORDER)		
	8	2" (BINDING)		

Storm at Sea Units

To make each unit, refer to the fabric key on page 48 and the illustrations that follow.

Unit A

1. Mark a sewing line on wrong side of the following 3½" squares.

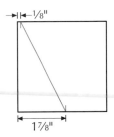 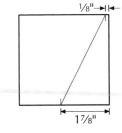

Mark from the left-hand edge:
16 dark pink
12 dark coral
12 dark purple
12 dark blue
100 light

Mark from the right-hand edge:
16 dark pink
12 dark coral
12 dark purple
12 dark blue
100 light

2. Following the directions on pages 8–10, piece A units. Make Unit A in 12 color schemes. For all A units, use 3½" x 6½" rectangles and the marked 3½" squares.

Unit A
Make 16 green #1, dark pink, and light.
Make 12 green #2, dark coral, and light.
Make 12 green #3, dark purple, and light.
Make 12 green #4, dark blue, and light.

Unit A
Make 3 each pink, dark pink,
coral, dark coral, blue, dark blue,
purple, and dark purple with
light background.

Unit C

Following the directions on pages 11–12, piece C units. Make Unit C in 8 color schemes. For all C units, use 3½" squares for the centers and 2" squares for the corners.

Unit C
Make 4 gold and dark pink.
Make 3 gold and dark coral.
Make 3 gold and dark blue.
Make 3 gold and dark purple.

Unit C
Make 6 each green #1,
#2, #3, and #4 with
light background.

Unit D and Unit D Variation

1. Cut the 3⅞" squares in half diagonally. You will have a total of 144 triangles.

2. Following the directions on page 12, piece D units. Make Unit D in 6 color schemes. For all D units, use 4¾" light print squares, 2⅝" squares, and the triangles from step 1.

Unit D
Make 4.

Unit D
Make 3.

Unit D
Make 3.

Unit D
Make 4.

Unit D
Make 1.

Unit D
Make 1.

3. Make the Unit D variation shown below in 4 color schemes. To make a simplified Unit D, use two 2⅝" squares per unit.

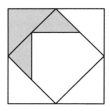

Partial Unit D
Make 6.

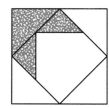

Partial Unit D
Make 6.

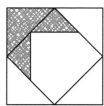

Partial Unit D
Make 4.

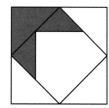

Partial Unit D
Make 4.

Quilt Top Assembly

Following the quilt plan, arrange the completed units, the remaining 3½" x 6½" light rectangles, and the 3½" light squares. Stitch the units together, referring to "Assembling the Quilt Top" on page 15. Press the joining seams open.

Borders

Refer to pages 74–76.

1. Measure, cut, mark, and attach the 2"-wide light inner borders to the quilt top, piecing as needed.

2. Add the 5"-wide floral outer borders to the quilt in the same way.

Quilt Finishing

Refer to pages 76–78.

1. Layer the quilt top with batting and backing; baste.

2. Quilt a design of your choice.

3. Piece binding strips together and bind quilt edges.

Regatta

Finished Size: 38½" x 46"

Finished Unit A Size: 2½" x 5"
Finished Unit C Sizes:
2½" x 2½" and 5" x 5"

Color Photo: Page 22

"Regatta" is based on the traditional Storm at Sea layout. Deleting some of the original design lines resulted in a fitting Storm at Sea adaptation.

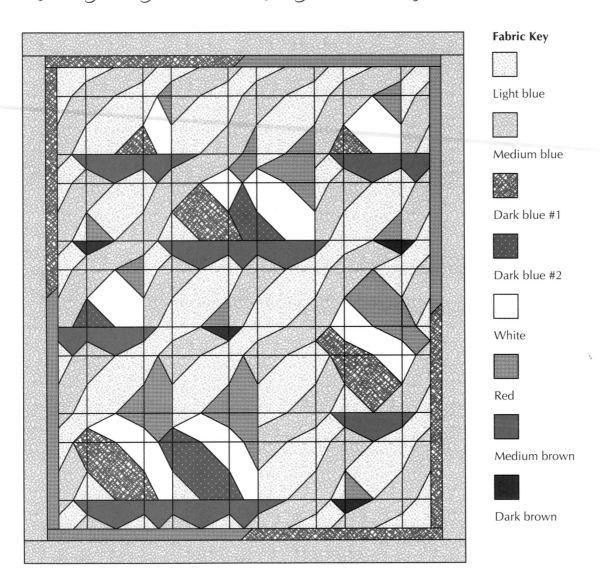

Fabric Key

Light blue

Medium blue

Dark blue #1

Dark blue #2

White

Red

Medium brown

Dark brown

Materials: 44"-wide fabric

1⅛ yds. light blue print
1⅓ yds. medium blue print for
   waves, outer border, and binding
⅔ yd. dark blue print #1
¼ yd. dark blue print #2

½ yd. white print
½ yd. red print
⅓ yd. medium brown print
¼ yd. dark brown print
1⅜ yds. for backing

Cutting Chart

FABRIC	FIRST CUT		SECOND CUT	
	NO. OF STRIPS	STRIP WIDTH	NO. OF PIECES	DIMENSIONS
LIGHT BLUE	2	5½"	12	5½" x 5½"
	7	3"	88	3" x 3"
			8	1¾" x 1¾"
MEDIUM BLUE	7	3"	31	3" x 5½"
			33	3" x 3"
	2	1¾"	38	1¾" x 1¾"
	4	2¼" (OUTER BORDER)		
	5	2" (BINDING)		
DARK BLUE #1	1	5½"	3	5½" x 5½"
	1	3"	11	3" x 3"
			1	1¾" x 1¾"
	4	1½" (INNER BORDER)		
DARK BLUE #2			1	5½" x 5½"
			1	3" x 5½"
			6	3" x 3"
			1	1¾" x 1¾"
WHITE	1	5½"	3	5½" x 5½"
	2	3"	11	3" x 3"
			6	3" x 5½"
			6	1¾" x 1¾"
RED	2	3"	3	3" x 5½"
			23	3" x 3"
	1	6"	1	5½" x 5½"
	CUT REMAINDER INTO FOUR 1½" STRIPS (INNER BORDER)			
			1	1¾" x 1¾"
MEDIUM BROWN	2	3"	8	3" x 5½"
			8	3" x 3"
	1	1¾"	8	1¾" x 1¾"
DARK BROWN			4	3" x 3"
			4	1¾" x 1¾"

Storm at Sea Units

To make each unit, refer to the fabric key on page 52 and the illustrations that follow. To help with assembly, each unit is designated by a letter and number. The letter refers to the horizontal row the unit is in, and the number refers to the vertical column. To arrange the units, use the Block Location Key below as you would a map. If you have extra space or a design wall, it may be easiest to put each unit in the correct place as you sew.

Partial Unit A

1. Mark a sewing line on the wrong side of the following 3" squares.

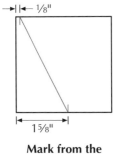

Mark from the left-hand edge:
2 medium blue
28 light blue
5 dark blue #1
2 dark blue #2
5 red
2 white
2 medium brown
2 dark brown

Mark from the right-hand edge:
8 medium blue
36 light blue
3 dark blue #1
2 dark blue #2
4 red
4 white
2 dark brown

2. Following the directions on page 10, piece partial A units. Make Unit A in 22 color schemes. For all A units, use 3" x 5½" rectangles and marked 3" squares.

A. *For the following partial A units, use 3" squares marked only from the left edge.*

Partial Unit A
Make 5 for
Blocks A2, A4,
A6, G6, and J6.

Partial Unit A
Make 1 for
Block A8.

Partial Unit A
Make 1 for
Block C4.

Partial Unit A
Make 1 for
Block E2.

Partial Unit A
Make 1 for
Block L6.

Partial Unit A
Make 1 for
Block L8.

Partial Unit A
Make 1 for
Block K3.

Partial Unit A
Make 1 for
Block K5.

B. *For the following partial A units, use 3" squares marked only from the right edge.*

Partial Unit A
Make 11 for Blocks B1, B9, D1, D3,
D7, D9, F3, F5, H1, K7, and K9.

Partial Unit A
Make 1 for
Block B5.

Partial Unit A
Make 1 for
Block B7.

Partial Unit A
Make 1 for
Block F1.

Partial Unit A
Make 2 for
Blocks F7 and H9.

Partial Unit A
Make 1 for Block G8.

C. *For the following partial A units, use two 3" squares marked from the left edge and one 3" square marked from the right edge.*

Partial Unit A
Make 1 for Block B3.

Partial Unit A
Make 1 for Block D5.

Partial Unit A
Make 2 for Blocks E8 and G4.

D. *For the following partial A units, use two 3" squares marked from the right-hand edge and one 3" square marked from the left-hand edge.*

Partial Unit A
Make 1 for
Block F9.

Partial Unit A
Make 2 for
Blocks H7 and K1.

Partial Unit A
Make 1 for
Block J2.

Partial Unit A
Make 1 for
Block J4.

E. *For the following partial A units, use one 3" square marked from the left edge and one 3" square marked from the right edge.*

Partial Unit A
Make 2 for Blocks H3 and H5.

Partial Unit A
Make 8 for Blocks C2, C8,
E4, E6, G2, J8, L2, and L4.

Partial Unit A
Make 1 for Block C6.

Partial Unit C

Following the directions on pages 11–12, piece C units. Unit C is made in 2 size variations, several piecing variations, and 24 color schemes.

A. *For the following partial C units, use 3" squares for the centers and 1¾" squares for the corners.*

Partial Unit C
Make 2 for
Blocks A1 and L9.

Partial Unit C
Make 1 for Block J5.

B. *For the following partial C units, use 3" squares for the centers and 1¾" squares for the corners.*

Partial Unit C
Make 1 for Block A3.

Partial Unit C
Make 3 for Blocks
A5, A7, and A9.

Partial Unit C
Make 6 for Blocks C3,
C9, E5, G1, L3, and L5.

Partial Unit C
Make 3 for Blocks
E7, G3, and J9.

Partial Unit C
Make 2 for Blocks
E9 and G5.

Partial Unit C
Make 1 for Block J1.

Partial Unit C
Make 1 for Block J3.

C. *For the following partial C units, use 3" squares for the centers and 1¾" squares for the corners.*

Partial Unit C
Make 5 for Blocks C1,
C7, E3, J7, and L1.

Partial Unit C
Make 1 for Block C5.

Partial Unit C
Make 2 for Blocks
E1 and L7.

Partial Unit C
Make 1 for Block G7.

Partial Unit C
Make 1 for Block G9.

D. *For the following partial C units, use 5½" squares for the centers and 3" squares for the corners.*

Partial Unit C
Make 1 for Block B2.

Partial Unit C
Make 4 for Blocks
B4, F6, H6, and K6.

Partial Unit C
Make 5 for Blocks B6,
D8, F4, H2, and H4.

Partial Unit C
Make 1 for Block B8.

Partial Unit C
Make 2 for Blocks
D2 and K8.

Partial Unit C
Make 1 for Block D4.

Partial Unit C
Make 1 for Block D6.

Partial Unit C
Make 1 for Block F2.

Partial Unit C
Make 1 for Block F8.

Partial Unit C
Make 1 for Block H8.

Partial Unit C
Make 1 for Block K4.

Partial Unit C
Make 1 for Block K2.

Quilt Top Assembly

Arrange the completed units following the quilt plan. Stitch the units together, referring to "Assembling the Quilt Top" on page 15. Press the joining seams open.

Borders

Refer to pages 74–76.

1. For each side inner border, join 1 red 1½" strip and 1 dark blue 1½" strip at a 45° angle as shown. Trim excess fabric and press.

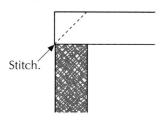

Side Border
Make 2.

2. Repeat for top and bottom inner borders, stitching in the opposite direction as shown.

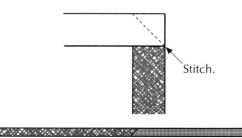

Top and Bottom Borders
Make 2.

3. Measure, cut, mark, and attach the pieced inner borders. The seam should be approximately in the center of each border.

4. Add the 2¼"-wide medium blue outer borders in the same way.

Quilt Finishing

Refer to pages 76–78.

1. Layer the quilt top with batting and backing; baste.

2. Quilt in-the-ditch and add any extra quilting as desired.

3. Piece binding strips together and bind quilt edges.

Dream Weaver

Finished Size: 35" x 42½"
Finished Unit A Size: 2½" x 5"
Finished Unit C Size: 2½" x 2½"
Finished Unit D Size: 5" x 5"

Color Photo: Page 23

"Dream Weaver" was designed on the Storm at Sea layout, but the use of color and value change the motion of the traditional pattern. Light and medium fabrics form a woven pattern against a dark background.

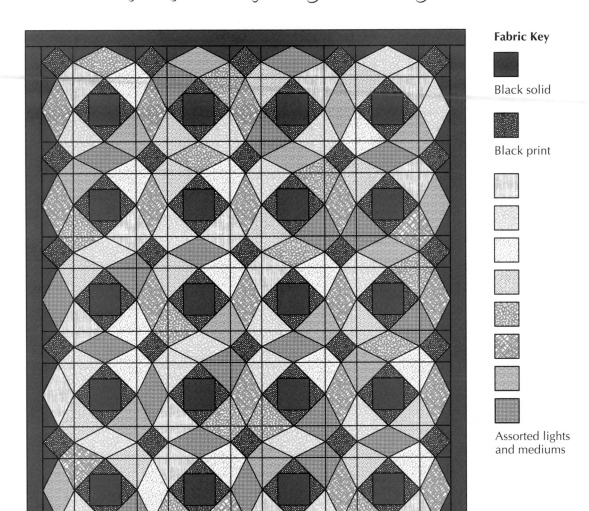

Fabric Key

Black solid

Black print

Assorted lights
and mediums

Materials: 44"-wide fabric

1 yd. black solid for blocks and
   outer border

1 yd. black print for blocks and
   binding

2¼ yards total assorted light and
medium prints in shades of
red, orange, purple, green,
blue, yellow, and pink
(approximately 30 fabrics in all)

1⅓ yds. for backing

Cutting Chart

FABRIC	FIRST CUT		SECOND CUT	
	No. of Strips	Strip Width	No. of Pieces	Dimensions
BLACK SOLID	2	4"	20	4" x 4"
	3	3"	36	3" x 3"
	2	1¾"	40	1¾" x 1¾"
	4	1½" (BORDER)		
BLACK PRINT	3	3"	30	3" x 3"
	5	2¼"	80	2¼" x 2¼"
	5	2" (BINDING)		
ASSORTED LIGHTS AND MEDIUMS			40	3⅜" x 3⅜"*
			160	3" x 3"
			80	1¾" x 1¾"
			49	3" x 5½"

*FOR EVERY 3⅜" SQUARE YOU CUT FROM THE SAME FABRIC, CUT TWO 1¾" SQUARES AND FOUR 3" SQUARES FROM THE SAME FABRIC.

Storm at Sea Units

To make each unit, refer to the fabric key on page 58 and the illustrations that follow.

IMPORTANT: All adjacent triangle corners must be of the same print. This requires careful planning. Do not construct all the units at once. Work one section at a time, moving diagonally across the quilt and referring often to the color photo on page 23.

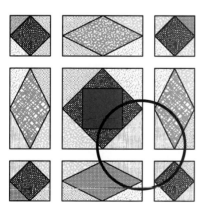

Same color must be used in adjacent corners.

To duplicate the look of the photo quilt exactly, additional planning is required. Certain colors repeat along the diagonal bands running from the upper left corner to the lower right corner. You might want to make a color diagram of the quilt and use it as a guide.

Unit A

1. Mark a sewing line on the wrong side of the following 3" squares.

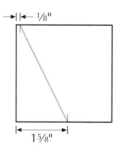
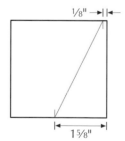

Mark from the left-hand edge:
80 assorted lights and mediums
18 black solid

Mark from the right-hand edge:
80 assorted lights and mediums
18 black solid

For each assorted fabric, mark half the squares from the left and half from the right. If you cut 8 squares, mark 4 from the left and 4 from the right.

2. Following the directions on pages 8–10, piece 1 Unit A at a time using the 3" x 5½" rectangles and the marked 3" squares.

>   **A.** *The following A units use four 3" squares of different fabrics.*

Unit A
Make 31.

>   **B.** *The following A units, which go around the edges of the design, use 2 assorted 3" squares of different fabrics and 2 black solid 3" squares.*

Unit A
Make 18.

Unit C

Following the directions on pages 11–12, piece 1 Unit C at a time. Make Unit C in 3 color schemes. For all C units, use 3" black print squares for the centers and 1¾" squares for the corners.

>   **A.** *The following C units use 4 assorted 1¾" squares of different fabrics.*

Unit C
Make 12.

>   **B.** *The following C units, which go around the edges of the design, use 2 assorted 1¾" squares of different fabrics and 2 black solid 1¾" squares.*

Unit C
Make 14.

>   **C.** *The following C units, which go in the corners of the design, use 1 assorted 1¾" square and 3 black solid 1¾" squares.*

Unit C
Make 4.

Unit D

1. Cut the 3⅜" assorted squares in half diagonally. You will have a total of 80 triangles.

2. Following the directions on page 12, piece 1 Unit D at a time using the 4" black solid squares, the 2¼" black-print squares, and the triangles from step 1.

Unit D
Make 20.

Quilt Top Assembly

Arrange the completed units following the quilt plan. Refer to the color photograph on page 23 for color placement, if desired. Stitch the units together, referring to "Assembling the Quilt Top" on page 15. Press the joining seams open.

Borders

Refer to pages 74–76.

Measure, cut, mark, and attach the 1½"-wide black solid borders to the quilt top.

Quilt Finishing

Refer to pages 76–78.

1. Layer the quilt top with batting and backing; baste.

2. Quilt in-the-ditch or quilt a design of your choice.

3. Piece binding strips together and bind quilt edges.

Field of Flowers

Several different fabrics were used for each flower color, and various shades of green give the leaves and stems a scrappy look. You could use fewer flower fabrics and just one green for the stems and leaves.

Finished Size: 43¾" x 55"
Finished Unit B Size: 2½" x 2½"
Finished Half-Square Triangle Unit Size: 2½" x 2½"
Finished Block Size: 6¼" x 7½"

Color Photo: Page 25

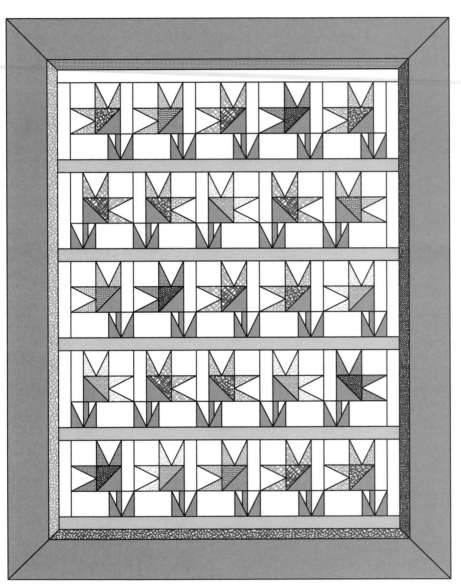

Fabric Key

Dark reds   Dark purples

Medium reds   Medium purples

Dark oranges   Golds

Medium oranges   Yellows

Dark pinks   Light blue

Medium pinks   Greens

Materials: 44"-wide fabric

¼ yd. dark red print #1
Scraps of 2 additional dark red prints (#2 and #3), each at least 4" x 4"

¼ yd. medium red print #1
⅛ yd. *each* 2 additional medium red prints (#2 and #3)
continued next page

Scraps of 2 different dark orange prints, each at least 4" x 4"

⅛ yd. *each* 2 different medium orange prints

Scraps of 3 different dark pink prints, each at least 4" x 4"

⅛ yd. *each* 3 different medium pink prints

¼ yd. dark purple print #1

Scrap of dark purple print #2, at least 4" x 4"

¼ yd. medium purple print #1

⅛ yd. medium purple print #2

Scraps of 3 different gold prints, each at least 4" x 4"

⅛ yd. *each* 3 different yellow prints

1½ yds. light blue print for background

¼ yd. *each* 5 different green prints for stems and leaves

⅓ yd. light green print for sashing

⅞ yd. medium green for outer border

2⅔ yds. for backing

Cutting Chart

FABRIC	FIRST CUT		SECOND CUT	
	NO. OF STRIPS	STRIP WIDTH	NO. OF PIECES	DIMENSIONS
DARK RED #1			1	3⅜" x 3⅜"
	1	1½" (BOTTOM INNER BORDER)		
DARK REDS #2 & #3			1* (2 TOTAL)	3⅜" x 3⅜"
MEDIUM RED #1	1	3"	8	3" x 3"
	2	1½" (SIDE INNER BORDER)		
MEDIUM REDS #2 & #3	1*	3"	8 (16 TOTAL)	3" x 3"
DARK ORANGES			1* (2 TOTAL)	3⅜" x 3⅜"
MEDIUM ORANGES	1*	3"	8 (16 TOTAL)	3" x 3"
DARK PINKS			1* (3 TOTAL)	3⅜" x 3⅜"
MEDIUM PINKS	1*	3"	8 (24 TOTAL)	3" x 3"
DARK PURPLE #1			1	3⅜" x 3⅜"
	2	1½" (SIDE INNER BORDER)		
DARK PURPLE #2			1	3⅜" x 3⅜"
MEDIUM PURPLE #1	1	3"	8	3" x 3"
	1	1½" (TOP INNER BORDER)		
MEDIUM PURPLE #2	1	3"	8	3" x 3"
GOLDS			1* (3 TOTAL)	3⅜" x 3⅜"
YELLOWS	1*	3"	8* (24 TOTAL; DISCARD 4 MATCHING)	3" x 3"
LIGHT BLUE	9	3"	75	3" x 3"
			25	3" x 4¼"
	9	1¾"	1	1¾" x 34¼"
			5	1¾" x 18"
			10	1¾" x 8"
			25	1¾" x 5½"
	3	1¼"	5	1¼" x 18"
GREENS			3* (15 TOTAL)	3⅜" x 3⅜"
	1*	3"	10* (50 TOTAL)	3" x 3"
	1	1"	1* (5 TOTAL)	1" x 18"
LIGHT GREEN	5	1¾"	5	1¾" x 34¼"
				(HORIZONTAL SASHING)
MEDIUM GREEN	6	4¼" (OUTER BORDER)		

*FROM EACH FABRIC

Storm at Sea Units

To make each unit, refer to the fabric key on page 62 and the illustrations that follow.

Unit B

1. Mark a sewing line on the wrong side of the 3" squares for the flowers and leaves.

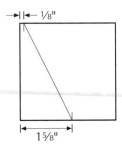

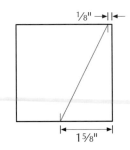

Mark from the left-hand edge:
12 medium red
8 medium orange
12 medium pink
8 medium purple
10 yellow
5 each of 5 different greens

Mark from the right-hand edge:
12 medium red
8 medium orange
12 medium pink
8 medium purple
10 yellow
5 each of 5 different greens

2. Following the directions on pages 10–11, piece B units using 3" light blue squares for the centers and the marked 3" flower-fabric squares for the points. Use the same flower fabric for both points in each unit and make 2 matching units for each flower.

Unit B
Make 12.

Unit B
Make 8.

Unit B
Make 12.

Unit B
Make 8.

Unit B
Make 10.

Unit B Variation (Stems and Leaves)

1. Stitch a 1¼" x 18" light blue strip to one long edge of a 1" x 18" green strip as shown. Stitch a 1¾" x 18" light blue strip to the other side. Make a total of 5 strip sets.

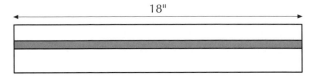

18"

2. Crosscut strip sets into a total of 25 squares, each 3" x 3", to make the background square.

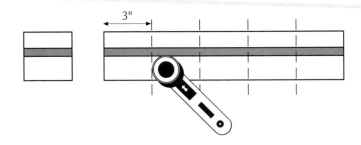

3"

3. Following the directions on pages 10–11, piece Unit B variations using the 3" pieced squares from step 2 and the marked 3" green squares for the points. Be sure to match the green fabrics within each unit. Make a total of 15 units with the stem on the left, and 10 units with the stem on the right as shown.

Unit B
Make 15.

Unit B
Make 10.

Half-Square Triangle Units

1. Cut the 3⅜" squares in half diagonally. You will have a total of 30 green and 26 dark flower-fabric triangles. Discard 1 gold triangle and 1 triangle from each green fabric.

2. Stitch each dark flower-fabric triangle to a green triangle, mixing fabrics randomly.

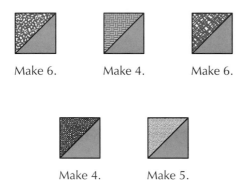

Make 6. Make 4. Make 6.

Make 4. Make 5.

Block Assembly

Stitch completed units, 3" light blue squares, 3" x 4¼" light blue rectangles, and 1¾" x 5½" light blue rectangles into blocks as shown. When piecing each block, make sure the green fabrics in the units match.

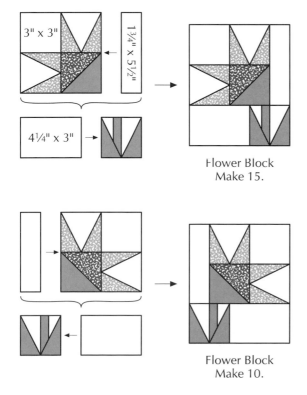

Flower Block
Make 15.

Flower Block
Make 10.

Quilt Top Assembly

1. Stitch Flower blocks into 5 rows of 5 blocks each. Make 3 rows with the flowers facing left and 2 rows with the flowers facing right. Add a 1¾" x 8" light blue strip to each end of each row as shown.

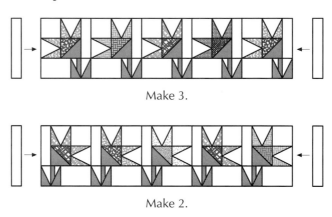

Make 3.

Make 2.

2. Join the rows to 1¾" x 34¼" light green sashing strips as shown.

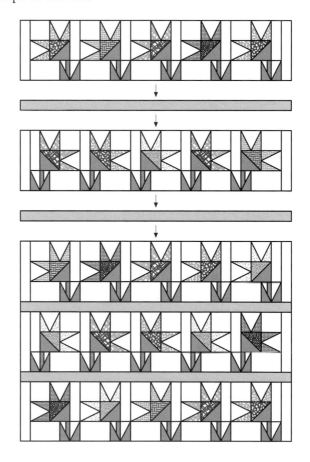

3. Stitch a 1¾" x 34¼" light green sashing strip to the bottom of the quilt. Stitch a 1¾" x 34¼" light blue sashing strip to the top of the quilt as shown.

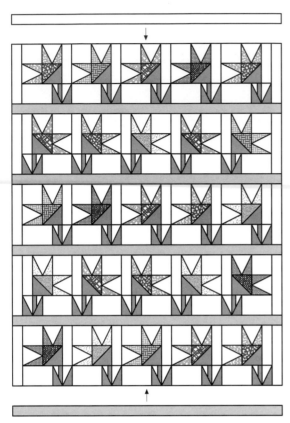

Borders

Refer to pages 74–76.

1. Join the 1½"-wide medium red border strips to make a 1½" x 58" strip. Repeat with the dark purple strips.

2. Join the 4¼"-wide medium green outer-border strips to make two 4¼" x 58" strips and two 4¼" x 47" strips.

3. Stitch the 1½"-wide medium red and dark purple inner-border strips to the 2 long outer-border strips. Stitch the 1½"-wide medium purple and dark red inner-border strips to the 2 short outer-border strips, matching the centers.

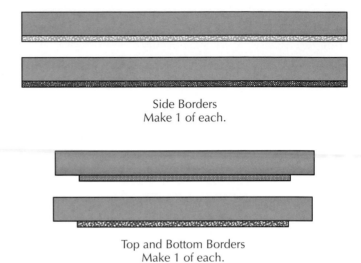

Side Borders
Make 1 of each.

Top and Bottom Borders
Make 1 of each.

4. Measure, mark, and pin the border strips to the quilt top. Sew the strips to the quilt top and miter the corners.

Quilt Finishing

Refer to pages 76–78.

1. Layer the quilt top with batting and backing; baste.

2. Quilt as desired.

3. Cut 2"-wide strips from the leftover flower fabrics. Piece with diagonal seams to make 1 strip, approximately 220" long. Bind the quilt edges.

Aquarius

Finished Size: 78" x 78"
Finished Unit B Size: 4" x 4"
Finished Four-Patch
Unit Size: 4" x 4"
Finished Half-Square Triangle
Unit Size: 4" x 4"
Finished Block Size: 12" x 12"

Color Photo: Page 27

"Aquarius" features a variety of light, medium, and dark prints. Light and medium fabrics predominate in the center of the quilt, changing to dark fabrics near the borders. It doesn't matter if you use just a few fabrics or many; value is most important. Study the photo for fabric placement.

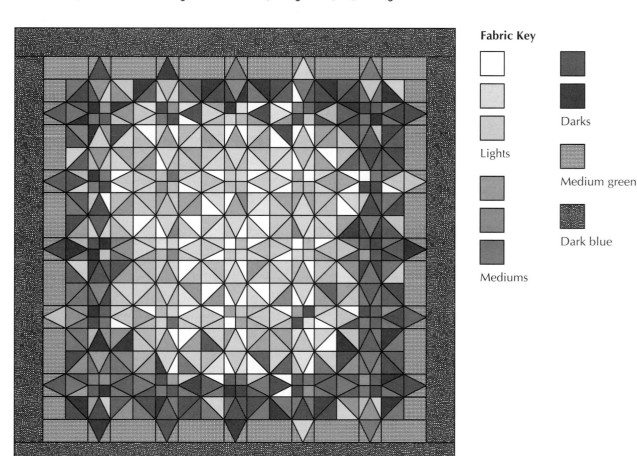

Fabric Key

Lights

Mediums

Darks

Medium green

Dark blue

Materials: 44"-wide fabric

7 yds. *total* assorted light, medium, and dark prints in shades of blue, green, tan, and ivory

1½ yds. medium green print for pieced border

1⅞ yds. dark blue print for outer border and binding

4⅔ yds. for backing

Cutting Chart

FABRIC	FIRST CUT		SECOND CUT	
	NO. OF STRIPS	STRIP WIDTH	NO. OF PIECES	DIMENSIONS
ASSORTED PRINTS	12	4⅞"	100	4⅞" x 4⅞"
	36	4½"	320	4½" x 4½"
	7	2½"	100	2½" x 2½"
MEDIUM GREEN	10	4½"	20	4½" x 8½"
			44	4½" x 4½"
DARK BLUE	8	5¼" (OUTER BORDER)		
	8	2" (BINDING)		

Storm at Sea Units

To make each unit, refer to the fabric key on page 67 and the illustrations that follow.

Unit B

1. Mark a sewing line on the wrong side of the following 4½" squares.

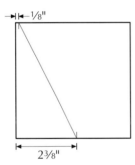
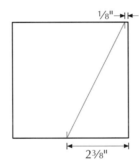

←|←—⅛"   ⅛"—→|←—

|←— 2⅜" —→| |←— 2⅜" —→|

Mark from the
left-hand edge:
100 assorted prints
20 medium green

Mark from the
right-hand edge:
100 assorted prints
20 medium green

2. Following the directions on pages 10–11, piece B units using both marked and unmarked 4½" assorted squares. Make 20 predominately light units, 10 predominately medium units, and 5 dark units. Make the remainder a combination of light, medium, and dark. You will have 20 unmarked squares left over for the border.

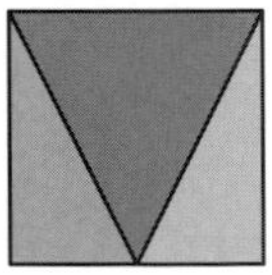

Unit B
Make 100.

Four-Patch Unit

Make four-patch units using the 2½" assorted squares. Make 3 predominately light units, 3 predominately medium units, and 3 dark units. Make the remainder a combination of light, medium, and dark.

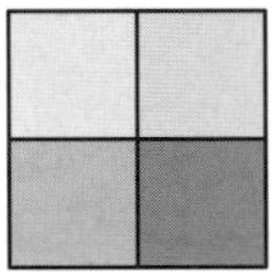

Four-Patch Units
Make 25.

Half-Square Triangle Unit

1. Cut the 4⅞" squares in half diagonally, from corner to corner (see the note below). You will have 200 triangles.

2. Stitch the triangles together to make half-square triangle units, mixing fabrics randomly.

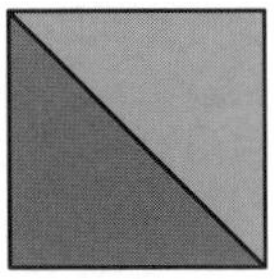

Make 100.

Note:

If you're in a hurry and don't mind a little less variety, do not cut the squares. Instead, follow the directions on page 13 for making Unit F. Each pair of squares will yield 2 units with the same 2 fabrics.

Block Assembly

Stitch the completed units together as shown. Make 25 blocks. Make at least 9 of these blocks from lighter-value units for the center of the quilt.

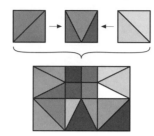

Quilt Top Assembly

1. Arrange the completed blocks, placing the lightest blocks in the center. Sew the blocks into 5 rows of 5 blocks each. Press the joining seams open.

2. Stitch the rows together to complete the quilt top. Press the joining seams open.

Borders

Refer to pages 74–76.

1. Following the directions on pages 10–11, piece B units for the inner border using the remaining 4½" assorted squares and the marked 4½" green squares. You will have 4 green squares left over for the corners.

Unit B
Make 20.

2. Stitch side borders as shown, using B units from step 1, 4½" x 8½" green rectangles, and the remaining 4½" green squares.

Side Borders
Make 2.

3. Stitch the top and bottom borders as shown, using B units from step 1 and 4½" x 8½" green rectangles.

Top and Bottom Borders
Make 2.

4. Stitch the side borders to the quilt, matching seams as necessary. Add top and bottom borders.

5. Join the 5¼"-wide blue strips as needed to make outer borders long enough for your quilt.

6. Measure the quilt top and cut borders the length needed.

7. Pin the outer border to the quilt. Add the side borders first, then the top and bottom borders.

Quilt Finishing

Refer to pages 76–78.

1. Layer the quilt top with batting and backing; baste.

2. Quilt as desired.

3. Piece binding strips together and bind quilt edges.

School of Fish

Two units are all you need to make this charming quilt. Blue fabrics ranging from light to dark create the illusion of a deep blue sea, home to tropical fish made from the liveliest fabrics in your scrap bag.

Finished Size: *44½" x 53"*
Finished Unit B Size: 3" x 3"
Finished Unit C Size: 3" x 3"
Finished Block Size: 6" x 6"

Color Photo: Page 26

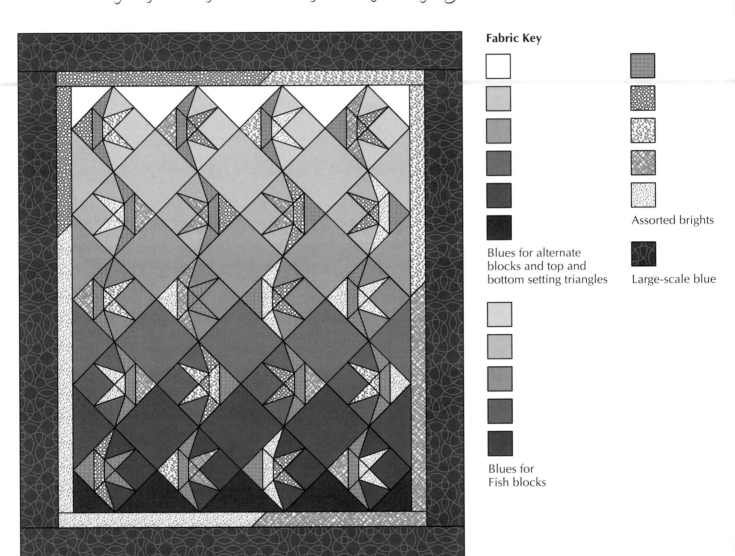

Fabric Key

Assorted brights

Blues for alternate
blocks and top and
bottom setting triangles

Large-scale blue

Blues for
Fish blocks

Materials: 44"-wide fabric

⅓ yd. lightest blue print (or a scrap, at least 10" x 16") for top setting triangles

⅓ yd. darkest blue print (or a scrap, at least 10" x 16") for bottom setting triangles

1¾ yds. total of at least 8 different assorted bright prints, including ¼ yd. *each* purple, pink, red, and gold prints

⅓ yd. *each* of 4 blue prints for Alternate blocks, in a range from medium light to medium dark

⅛ yd. *each* of 5 blue prints for Fish blocks, in a range from light to dark

1 yd. large-scale blue print for outer border and binding

2⅔ yds. for backing

Cutting Chart

FABRIC	FIRST CUT		SECOND CUT	
	NO. OF STRIPS	STRIP WIDTH	NO. OF PIECES	DIMENSIONS
LIGHTEST BLUE			1	9¾" x 9¾"
			1	5⅛" x 5⅛"
DARKEST BLUE			1	9¾" x 9¾"
			1	5⅛" x 5⅛"
ALTERNATE BLUES	1*	9¾"	1* (4 TOTAL)	9¾" x 9¾"
		TRIM REMAINDER TO 6½"	3* (12 TOTAL)	6½" x 6½"
FISH BLUES	1*	3½"	12* (60 TOTAL)	3½" x 3½"
ASSORTED BRIGHTS			120	3½" x 3½"
			20	2" x 2"
PURPLE, PINK, RED, AND GOLD	2*	2" (INNER BORDER)		
LARGE-SCALE BLUE	5	4" (OUTER BORDER)		
	6	2" (BINDING)		

*FROM EACH FABRIC

Storm at Sea Units

Sew each Fish block separately, following the illustration below and the color photograph on page 26. The fish colors vary, and the background fabric is different in each row.

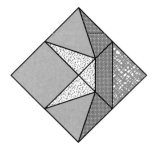

Fish Block
Make 20.

Unit B

B units form the fins and tails of the fish.

1. Mark a sewing line on the wrong side of the following 3½" assorted bright squares. From each fabric you use for the fins and tails, mark an equal number of squares from the right and left sides.

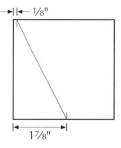

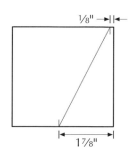

Mark from the left-hand edge:
40 assorted brights

Mark from the right-hand edge:
40 assorted brights

2. Following the directions on pages 10–11, piece B units using the 3½" blue background squares and the marked 3½" bright squares. For each fish, make 2 units with the same 2 bright fabrics and the same blue background fabric. For each row of fish, make 8 units (4 matching pairs) with the same background fabric (see photo on page 26).

Unit B
Make 20
(1 for each fish block).

Unit B
Make 20
(1 for each fish block).

Unit C Variation

C units form the head and body of the fish. Following the directions on pages 11–12, piece C units. For this C unit, use a 3½" square for the center, a 2" square for one corner, and a 3½" square for the opposite corner.

Unit C variation
Make 20 (1 for each fish block).

Note:
In the quilt on page 26, most of the fish bodies are made from the same fabrics as the fins and tails. The heads are made from a different fabric.

Block Assembly

Join the completed units and 3½" blue squares.

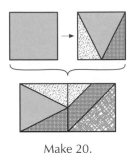

Make 20.

Quilt Top Assembly

1. Cut the 9¾" blue squares in half *twice* diagonally, for a total of 24 side setting triangles.

2. Cut the 5⅛" blue squares in half diagonally, for a total of 4 corner setting triangles.

3. Following the quilt plan, arrange the Fish blocks, 6½" alternate blue squares, and triangles. You will have several side setting triangles left over.

4. Sew the blocks together in diagonal rows as shown. Press the seam allowances in each row in opposite directions. Join the rows. Press.

Borders

Refer to pages 74–76.

1. For the side inner borders, join a 2"-wide pink strip to a 2"-wide red strip at a 45° angle as shown. Join a purple and a gold strip in the same way.

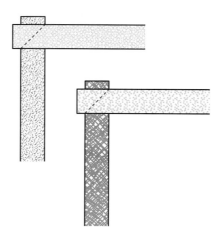

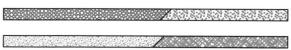

Side Borders
Make 1 of each.

2. For the top and bottom inner borders, join a 2" pink strip to a 2" purple strip at a 45° angle as shown. Join a red and a gold strip in the same way.

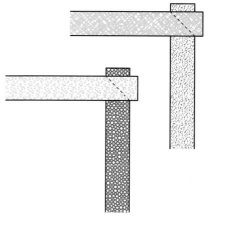

Top and Bottom Borders
Make 1 of each.

3. Measure, cut, mark, and attach the pieced inner borders. The seam should be approximately in the center of each border.

4. Add the 4" large-scale blue outer borders to the quilt in the same way, piecing as needed.

Quilt Finishing

Refer to pages 76–78.

1. Layer the quilt top with batting and backing; baste.

2. Quilt as desired.

3. Piece binding strips together and bind quilt edges.

Finishing Techniques

Borders

I make borders by cutting strips across the full width of the fabric, then joining them end to end to get the necessary length. Piecing borders saves fabric, and cutting crosswise strips is convenient, since you do the rest of your rotary cutting this way.

Straight-Cut Borders

1. Measure the length of the quilt top through the center. Cut 2 border strips to this measurement. If the quilt measures more than the width of the fabric, piece strips to the required length.

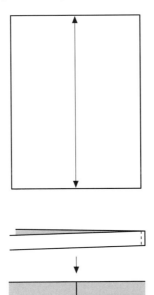

Piece borders if necessary.

2. Fold each border strip in half, then in half again. Mark the folds with pins as shown. Mark both sides of the quilt top in the same manner.

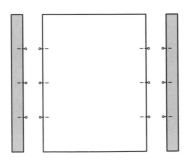

3. Pin borders to the sides of the quilt top, matching the markings and the outside edges. Ease in fullness if necessary. Stitch the side borders to the quilt. Press the seams toward the border.

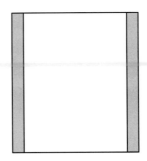

4. Measure the width of the quilt top through the center. Include the side borders in your measurement. Cut 2 border strips to this measurement. Piece the borders if necessary. Repeat steps 2 and 3 for top and bottom borders.

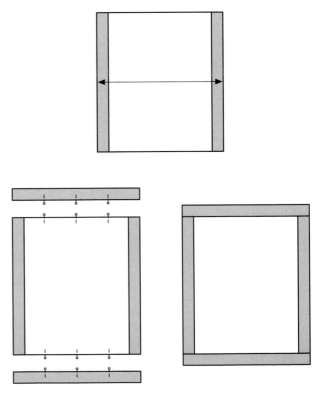

5. Repeat the above steps for any additional borders.

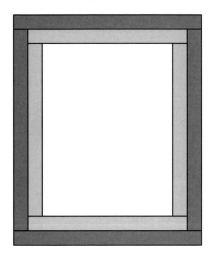

Mitered Borders

1. Measure the length and width of the quilt top through the center. Add twice the finished border width plus 2" to 3" to each measurement. Cut borders to this length. For example, if your quilt top measures 30" x 40" and your finished border width is 5", you would cut 53"-long strips for the side borders (40 + 5 + 5 + 3 = 53) and 43"-long strips for the top and bottom borders (30 + 5 + 5 + 3 = 43).

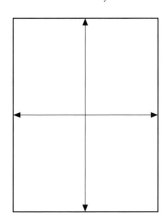

Add twice the finished border width plus 2" to 3" to these measurements.

2. On the wrong side of the quilt top, mark a ¼"-wide seam allowance on all 4 corners. Fold the quilt in half lengthwise and crosswise and mark the center of each side with a pin.

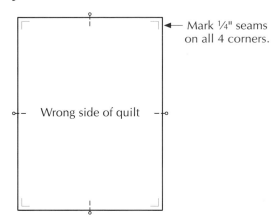

Mark ¼" seams on all 4 corners.

Wrong side of quilt

3. Fold each border strip in half lengthwise and mark the center with a pin. On the side borders, measure half the *length* of the quilt top from each side of the center. Mark these points with pins as shown. Repeat for the top and bottom borders, measuring half the *width* of the quilt top.

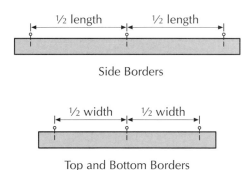

½ length   ½ length

Side Borders

½ width   ½ width

Top and Bottom Borders

4. Pin a border strip to the quilt top with right sides together and the quilt top uppermost. Match center points and the pins at each end of the border strip with the outside edges of the quilt top. Stitch the border to the quilt. Begin and end stitching exactly at the ¼" corner marks on the quilt top. Press seams toward the border. Repeat this procedure for all the remaining borders.

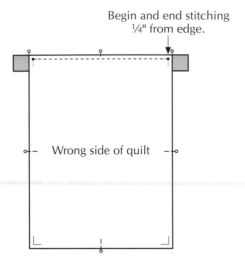

Begin and end stitching
¼" from edge.

Wrong side of quilt

from the border seam to the outside edge. Trim seam allowances to ¼". Press seams open or to one side.

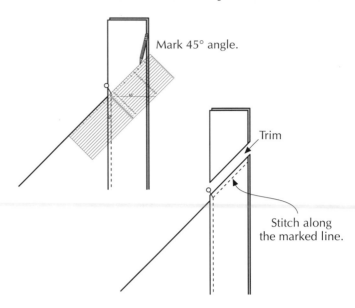

Mark 45° angle.

Trim

Stitch along
the marked line.

5. Working on one corner at a time, fold the quilt diagonally, right sides together. Make sure the long edges of the two borders line up. Insert a pin at the end of the border seam, pinning through all layers.

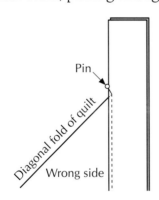

Pin

Diagonal fold of quilt

Wrong side

6. Align the 45°-angle line on your ruler with the border seam, placing the edge of the ruler exactly at the pin as shown above right. Mark the 45° angle on the border. Pin and stitch on the marked line. Stitch

Quilt Finishing

Basting

1. Make a backing that is several inches larger than the quilt top. Spread the backing on a flat surface, wrong side up. Anchor it with masking tape or clips.

2. Position the batting on top of the backing. Place the quilt on top of the batting, right side up. Baste all 3 layers together, starting at the center of the quilt and working out toward the edges. For hand quilting, baste in a lengthwise and crosswise grid approximately 6" to 8" apart. Baste along outside edges of quilt.

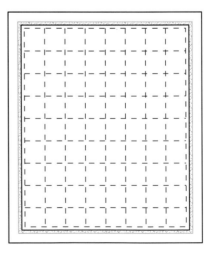

If you plan to machine quilt, use safety pins to hold the layers together instead of basting with thread.

Quilting

You can hand or machine quilt your Storm at Sea quilts. I have used both methods for the quilts in this book. Quilting in-the-ditch and continuous straight-line quilting are two good ways to emphasize the curvy motion of Storm at Sea designs.

If you are not familiar with quilting methods, I recommend that you consult one of the many fine books available on the subject. Try *Loving Stitches: A Guide to Fine Hand Quilting* by Jeana Kimball, *Quilting Makes the Quilt* by Lee Cleland, and *Machine Quilting Made Easy* by Maurine Noble (all from That Patchwork Place, Inc.).

Binding

1. Cut straight-grain binding strips across the full width of the fabric. I cut binding strips 2" wide. This gives the quilt a narrow finished edge.

2. To make the binding long enough to go around the quilt, sew the strips together, end to end, with 45° diagonal seams.

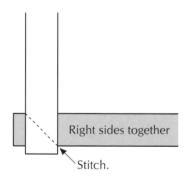

3. Press the strip in half lengthwise, right side out.

4. Fold the corner of the strip up at one end to form a 45° angle.

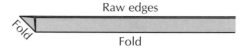

5. Place a pin ¼" from the outside edge on all 4 corners of the quilt top as shown.

6. Beginning with the folded corner, lay the binding strip on the quilt top with raw edges even. Stitch the binding to the quilt with a ¼"-wide seam allowance. Stop stitching at the corner pin, ¼" from the edge of the quilt. Cut the threads and remove the quilt from the sewing machine.

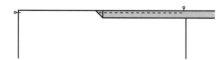

7. Fold the binding strip up, forming a right angle at the inner corner as shown.

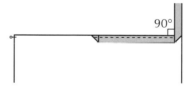

Fold the strip back down along the next side of the quilt top, aligning the fold with the side you just stitched. Beginning at the top edge, stitch the binding to the side of the quilt. End the stitching at the corner pin, ¼" from the edge of the quilt. Repeat this step for all 4 corners.

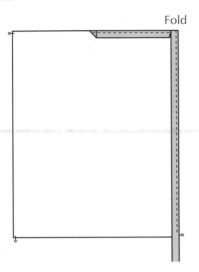

Fold

8. Overlap the binding by approximately ½" where the ends meet. Trim any excess, making a diagonal cut parallel to the folded edge at the beginning of the binding strip as shown. Fold the binding over to the back of the quilt and hand stitch in place, mitering each corner.

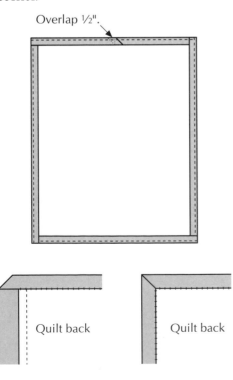

Overlap ½".

Quilt back   Quilt back

About the Author

MICHAEL SALSBURY

For as long as she can remember, Lydia Quigley has been making things. Besides sewing and knitting, she has tried weaving, rug hooking, stitchery, and painting. All these pursuits were relegated to the back of the closet when she discovered quilting in 1976.

In addition to making quilts, Lydia lectures and teaches workshops throughout Ontario. Her quilts have won many awards and have been exhibited throughout Canada, the United States, and Japan. In 1994 she started her own pattern company, The Rabbit Factory, which specializes in folk-art appliqué patterns.

Lydia lives in Kingston, Ontario, Canada, and is the mother of two teenagers.

Design Grid © Lydia Quigley

See "Designing Storm at Sea Quilts" on page 16.

Publications and Products

Many titles are available at your local quilt shop.
For more information, write for a free color catalog
to Martingale & Company, PO Box 118, Bothell,
WA 98041-0118 USA.

☎ U.S. and Canada, call **1-800-426-3126** for the
name and location of the quilt shop nearest you.
Int'l: 1-425-483-3313   **Fax:** 1-425-486-7596
E-mail: info@patchwork.com
Web: www.patchwork.com   1.98